COURS & ENTRAÎNEMENT

prépabac

Tle GÉNÉRALE

NOUVEAU BAC

Anglais LLCE

SPÉCIALITÉ

- **Christine Bitaillou**
  Professeure certifiée d'anglais
- **Viridiana Courty**
  Professeure agrégée d'anglais
- **Lucien Dubuisson**
  Professeur agrégé d'anglais
- **Isabelle Kherbouche**
  Professeure certifiée d'anglais

Hatier

Le site de vos révisions

L'achat de ce Prépabac vous permet de bénéficier d'un **ACCÈS GRATUIT*** à toutes les **ressources** d'annnabac.com (fiches, quiz, sujets corrigés…) et à ses **parcours de révision** personnalisés.

Pour profiter de cette offre, rendez-vous sur **www.annabac.com** dans la rubrique « Je profite de mon avantage client ».

* Selon les conditions précisées sur le site.

Maquette de principe : Frédéric Jély
Mise en pages : Soft office
Iconographie : Sophie Suberbere, Hatier Illustration
Édition : Olivier Martin

 ISBN 978-2-401-06459-1

AVANT-PROPOS

VOUS ÊTES EN TERMINALE générale, vous avez choisi la spécialité anglais LLCE et vous savez que la réussite dans cette matière demande un travail tout au long de l'année ? Cet ouvrage est pour vous !

Spécialement conçu pour vous accompagner dans vos apprentissages et vos révisions, il vous propose un ensemble de ressources très complet :

- des fiches de cours visuelles
- des cartes mentales récapitulatives
- des exercices progressifs
- des sujets de bac guidés
- des corrigés détaillés

Vous y trouverez tous les outils nécessaires pour mémoriser les connaissances clés sur les thématiques et les axes d'étude du programme et acquérir progressivement les méthodes de la synthèse, de la traduction et de la présentation du dossier oral.

Nous vous recommandons de l'utiliser régulièrement, en fonction de vos besoins. Ainsi, vous pourrez aborder les épreuves finales en toute sérénité, et acquérir les compétences nécessaires à la poursuite de vos études.

Les auteurs

Christine Bitaillou

Viridiana Courty

Lucien Dubuisson

Isabelle Kherbouche

SOMMAIRE

Les thématiques du programme

1 Art forms and debates of ideas

2 Expression and construction of the self

3 Travels, territories, frontiers

Les épreuves du bac

4 Faire une synthèse de documents

5 Améliorer son expression

6 Traduire un texte en français

7 Réussir l'épreuve orale

Annexes

Les thématiques du programme

1 Art forms and debates of ideas

Angela Davis was chosen for the poster as she is an icon of the fight for equality. She was an American Civil Rights activist in the 1960s and she is now fighting to end sex-based discrimination.

1 Denouncing oppression

En bref *Art and protest are intertwined: art has always been used as a medium to convey dissent. In some cases, art has allowed to expose social injustice and the excesses of power structures. In what ways can art become a tool to denounce the failures of society?*

I Artists and war

1 War poetry

- During World War I, many British writers were sent to the front. During his time in France, Wilfred Owen **described the atrocities of war** in some of his poems. "Anthem for Doomed Youth" (1917) laments the loss of young soldiers by depicting their deaths on the battle field and the mourning of their families.
- Owen's point of view contrasts with the position of other poets like Thomas Hardy who were employed by the British government to write and publish **patriotic poems**. The latter poets glorified the war and introduced soldiers as heroes dedicating themselves to their country.

2 The counterculture

- The counterculture was an **anti-war movement from the 1960s and 1970s**. Artists associated to the counterculture were openly opposed to US military intervention in Vietnam. For instance, "Give Peace a Chance" (1969) by the British band The Beatles became the anthem against the Vietnam War (1955-1975).
- The **Woodstock festival** (1969) is now seen as a decisive turning point in the counterculture: it promoted peace and showcased **artists who actively campaigned against the war in Vietnam**, such as Joan Baez, who is known for her political songs. Joan Baez even travelled to Vietnam in 1972, three years before the end of the war, in order to report on human rights conditions.

II Fighting oppressive governments

1 Denouncing totalitarianism

- After World War II, several European artists voiced concern about the expansion of the Soviet power in Eastern Europe and their fear that dictatorships would develop all over Europe. George Orwell, a British writer, was one of the strongest opponents to the Soviet power. The **dystopian** genre allowed him and other writers such as Ray Bradbury to **criticise the Soviet Union's repressive Communist regime** at the onset of the Cold War.

> **INFO**
> **Dystopian** literature introduces frightening worlds that have roots in existing societies such as totalitarian regimes.

- In his novel *1984* (1949), Orwell describes policies and techniques used by a dictatorship in a close future. Big Brother is the leader of Oceania and the subject of a cult of personality, though it is not sure he even is a real person. His face is made omnipresent through numerous posters and a network of "telescreens". This fictitious system of audiovisual devices illustrates the merging (*intrication*) of propaganda and surveillance in a totalitarian regime.

2 | Condemning colonialism

- After the decolonisation of African countries, many authors denounced the harmful consequences of colonisation. Chinua Achebe, from Nigeria, was one of the first African authors to be recognised internationally.
- His "African trilogy": *Things Fall Apart* (1958), *No Longer at Ease* (1960) and *Arrow of God* (1964) is an account of the disruption of Nigerian life and traditions caused by the arrival of British colonisers and religious missionaries in the end of the 19th century. The series goes on to depict the struggle of Nigerians who receive a British education and who are torn between their origins and the colonisers' mode of life.

zoOm

Nelson's Ship in a Bottle

Yinka Shonibare, *Nelson's Ship in a Bottle*, 2010.

In this art piece, Shonibare recreated British Admiral Nelson's ship. However, the sails are made with fabric and patterns associated with African dress and identity. Shonibare here denounces the glorification of Nelson, a fervent defender of slavery and colonialism in the 18th century.

→ Discover more about Nelson's Ship in a Bottle on the Royal Museums Greenwich website: bit.ly/PbacAngTle_1a

2 Fighting for a fairer world

En bref *Through their creations, artists may express their ideas and rally public opinion to their cause. Art is often what unites people, with artists giving momentum to a cause they believe in. How can art provoke social change?*

I Revealing social inequalities

1 Representing the upper class

- Satire is a genre used to mock and debunk people or ideas. Examples include Grayson Perry's tapestry *The Upper Class at Bay* (2012). Perry depicts an upper-class couple walking through their estate and dealing with protesters, and being submerged by taxes represented by stones. By using upper-class codes (the mansion, the deer hunt, etc.) Perry mocks the upper class's complaints that the government imposes too many taxes on them.
- In a contrary fashion, Evelyn Waugh mourns the decline of the English aristocracy in *Brideshead Revisited* (1945), a novel set in the prestigious University of Oxford. As opposed to Perry's work, this novel is an example of reactionary art: Waugh wishes things would go back to the way they were.

2 Exposing poverty and social issues

- In contemporary art, artists such as Ken Loach, Mierle Laderman Ukeles or Ron English are highly interested in the discrepancy between social classes. Ken Loach is known for his socially engaged movies which deal with low-paid jobs, unemployment, homelessness, and access to welfare.
- By focusing on the daily lives of normal people, Loach denounces the failure of the state to provide help. For instance, *I, Daniel Blake* (2016) follows a sick unemployed man as he fights to get an employment allowance from the state after his doctor tells him he can no longer work because of a heart condition.

II Fighting against discrimination

1 Condemning racism

- One of the leading authors in the fight against racism was Toni Morrison. Her 1987 novel *Beloved* throws light on the lives of former slaves after the **American Civil War**. Through her characters, she explores the issues of identity, or more precisely, the loss of identity of slaves.

INFO
The **American Civil War** opposed Northern states to Southern states on the question of slavery. The North eventually won and slavery was abolished in 1865.

■ Artists can call on people to react, just as Keith Haring with his lithograph *Free South Africa* (1985), attacking the racial segregation regime of apartheid. The comic-like image depicts a chained but tall South African rising against a small white oppressor and resembles an instruction guide for liberation.

2 | Denouncing sexism

■ Feminist figures include Angela Davis, an American civil rights activist. She was also a radical feminist during the counterculture movement and she later contributed to the development of feminist studies in several universities. She was more recently involved in the 2017 Women's March on Washington which protested against the election of Donald Trump as president of the United States.

■ Another feminist activist is Maya Angelou. She wrote several feminist poems such as "Still I Rise", "Caged Bird" and "Phenomenal Woman". In "Phenomenal Woman" (1978), she portrays a strong female figure who describes her body parts and the reaction of men to it. By doing so, she shows she is proud of her own body and claims it as her own. She demonstrates that the female body is not an object to be gazed at by male viewers.

zoOm

Protesting Trump's America

Margaret Atwood's *The Handmaid's Tale* (1985) regained popularity in Trump's America thanks to its TV adaption and its dystopian challenge of patriarchy. Protesters have taken up the novel's specific outfit to denounce legislation repressing women's rights.

→ Watch the trailer of the series: bit.ly/PbacAngTle_2a

3 Challenging taboos and myths

En bref *Artists can choose to represent a reality that is concealed in order to overturn social norms. However, artworks can be met by public outrage or even censorship. How can the representation of a hidden truth help artists to challenge taboos and myths?*

I Breaking taboos

1 Questionning moral codes

Though a critically acclaimed novel, J.D. Salinger's *The Catcher in the Rye* (1951) was met with outrage when it was published in the United States. It deals with identity in the formative teenage years and thus includes vulgar language, allusions to sex, smoking and alcohol. The novel defies family values by disrupting good social manners in order to emphasise the society's lack of depth. The book was first often banned from school libraries and teachers were not allowed to study it in class.

2 Defying sexual repression

- In D.H. Lawrence's *Lady Chatterley's Lover*, the story revolves around the affair between a married upper-class woman and a gamekeeper. The original novel made explicit use of sexual vocabulary and a censored version was published in Great Britain in 1932. However, the full novel was eventually made available in 1960: this led **Penguin Books** to be put on trial for publishing obscene material. Penguin's victory in the trial is often seen as the beginning of the permissive society and of the sexual revolution in Britain.

> **INFO**
> **Penguin Books** is an iconic British publishing house. They are famous for their editions of classic novels or collections in paperback edition (*livre de poche*).

- If Lawrence knowingly risked censorship, it was not the case of E.M. Forster. At a time when homosexuality was still illegal, he feared public reaction to *Maurice*, whose central topic is the hero's love for his college friend Clive. Forster only allowed a posthumous publication: written in 1913, his novel was published in 1971.

II Challenging offical history

1 Rewriting the westward expansion

- Artists can also challenge national myths that have been perpetuated in part by other artists. For instance, traditional Westerns from the first half of the 20th century represented the myth of westward expansion: Americans were portrayed as pioneers discovering empty lands and bringing civilisation to the west whereas Native Americans were depicted as bloodthirsty savages.

■ Arthur Penn's *Big Little Man* (1970) can then be called a revisionist Western, as it creates empathy for Native Americans and does not portray them as animals, like previous Westerns did. On the contrary, it is the US military which are portrayed as savages massacring the Native American population. By challenging the Hollywoodian codes of the Western, Penn challenged the national myth of the expansion of the United States.

2 | Documenting the truth

> **INFO**
> In 1942, Japanese aircrafts bombed the US naval base at **Pearl Harbor** in Hawaii. This attack marks the entry of the USA in World War II.

■ After the **attack on Pearl Harbor**, the US government decided to send Japanese-American citizens to concentration camps. Dorothea Lange was employed by the government to document the decent treatment of the population in those camps but her photographs in fact emphasised the forceful nature of the relocation, they were therefore impounded (*confisquées*) by the army. This allowed the government to publish anti-Japanese propaganda.

■ The photographs were only made public in the 1970s. By showing the exclusion of the population from American society, the photographs initiated Japanese American activism, and also allowed the collective memory of the war to include this dark chapter of history.

zoOm

Ignorance = Fear

Keith Haring, *Ignorance = Fear*, 1989.

In this work, Haring denounces misconceptions about AIDS patients. He rises up against the taboos surrounding AIDS and encourages patients and non-patients to be vocal about their condition in order to expose the falseness of stereotypes and stop discrimination.

→ Find out more about Haring's work to denounce the public's reaction to AIDS: bit.ly/PbacAngTle_3a

4 Breaking the rules of art

En bref *If art can be used as a weapon to challenge society and politics, it can turn on itself as well. Since the beginning of the 20th century, many artists have worked with art forms in order to modernise art. To what extent has art been modernised by artistic movements?*

I Emancipating from a traditional definition of art

1 The artistic avant-garde

- The term "avant-garde" is used to refer to **artists who experimented with their art form in order to create new boundaries**. Examples of avant-garde artistic movements include Cubism, Futurism and pop art. In 1914 in poetry, Imagism led the way for modernism. Poets such as Ezra Pound, Hilda Doolittle, and T.E. Hulme focused on fleeting moments such as a train coming into a station, a leaf falling, etc. Imagist poets believed that everything could be beautiful and they wanted to glorify and reproduce everyday moments. They wrote short poems of a few lines to reproduce the brief nature of their subjects. Their work thus completely differed from the long lyrical poems of Romantic poets.
- In American painting, **abstract expressionism** emerged after World War II with Jackson Pollock and Willem de Kooning. The subjects of their paintings are never easily discernible as they use the dripping method popularised by Pollock.

2 Contemporary forms of art

- In the late 1980s in the United Kingdom, a new group of artists emerged: the Young British Artists. The YBAs include visual artists such as Damien Hirst and Tracey Emin. Their goal was to move away from the search for beauty in art to an art form that shocks viewers by using unpleasant imagery.
- They also **challenged the very definition of the art form**: they moved away from traditional forms of visual art (paintings, photographies, collages) to include performance art and different objects. For instance, one of the most striking artworks from the YBAs is Hirst's *The Physical Impossibility of Death in the Mind of Someone Living* (1991): a dead shark in a glass tank filled with formaldehyde.

II Art in the consumer society

1 The banalisation of art

- With pop artists such as **Andy Warhol**, art further moved away from its traditions. Pop art is a criticism of the consumer society through artworks in which everyday objects are incorporated. For instance, Warhol depicted thirty-two cans of soup in *Campbell's Soup Cans* (1962) for the thirty-two flavours offered by the brand.

■ This type of work allowed a questioning of the nature of art: art was not elitist and elevated anymore, it could be involved and revolve around popular culture and everyday life.

2 Denouncing the commodification of art

■ Artists can also choose to be polemical, such as street artist Banksy. While in New York in October 2013, he installed a small stall close to Central Park, where an anonymous man was selling unidentified spray paintings for sixty dollars. Banksy later revealed he was the artist, making these artworks suddenly much more valuable. Through this stunt, he participated in the deconsecration of art: art is to be accessible and consumed by everyone, not just by wealthy privileged collectors in museums.

■ Banksy's critique went further in 2018 when his 2006 piece, *Girl with a Balloon*, self-shredded while it was sold at **Sotheby's**. The artist explained that he did not want his art sold at auction and that he built the shredding system to make sure the art piece would be destroyed if it was ever to become part of the art business.

INFO
Sotheby's is an auction house in the UK and the US. It is famous for auctioning artworks, collectibles, real estate and jewellery to wealthy buyers.

zoOm

Wyndham Lewis, *The Crowd*

Wyndham Lewis's painting is a great representation of the Vorticist movement's break with traditions: he interposes vertical and horizontal elements on a flat surface while the people in the crowd are drawn as red stick figures. The line of sight is also broken as the viewer can see elements from a worm's-eye view as well as a bird's-eye view. This creates a harshly drawn topsy-turvy world in which the stick figures appear to be lost.

→ Learn more about Vorticism on the Tate's website: bit.ly/PbacAngTle_4e

Wyndham Lewis, *The Crowd*, 1915.

5 The powerfulness of words

En bref *Public speaking allows people to make arguments through the use of words, whether in a speech or an exchange. Words can be a double-edge weapon: they can either inspire people to strive for a better world, or they can become dangerous tools of propaganda. In both cases, words become a weapon for politicians. How can words be manipulated to convince?*

I Unifying political speeches

1 Rallying a nation

■ Powerful speeches from eminent political figures often stay in collective memory. Former Prime Minister Winston Churchill was known for his uplifting speeches that brought the population together during World War II. He presented the retreat of the troops from Dunkirk in 1940 as a victory to strengthen British morale in his historic "We shall fight on the beaches" speech (June 1940). During the **Battle of France**, Churchill also delivered two other famous speeches: "Blood, toil, tears and sweat" and "This was their finest hour".

INFO
During the invasion of France, German troops pushed Allied forces (French, Belgian and British) to retreat to Dunkirk and to evacuate by the sea.

■ Another example would be American president John Fitzgerald Kennedy whose September 1962 speech "We choose to go to the Moon", in Houston, initiated public support for the Apollo program which eventually led to the Apollo 11 mission landing on the moon seven years later. His goal was to launch a national effort to win the space race by defining space as "the new frontier" that America needed to conquer. → FICHE 14

2 Fighting for civil rights

■ One of the most famous orators in the U.S. was Martin Luther King. He was the leading figure of the Civil Rights Movement, which fought for the end of segregation and equal rights for African-Americans. He made his "I Have a Dream" speech in front of more than 200,000 people at the March on Washington for Jobs and Freedom in 1963.

■ As Martin Luther King was a preacher, he often used allusions to religious elements, promoting acceptance in his speeches which were made even more powerful as it allowed him to appeal to his audience's emotions and beliefs. "I Have a Dream" is still remembered today as a greatly inspiring speech that marked an entire generation.

II Division and domination through words

1 Defending controversial opinions

- If words can be unifying, they can create division. In 1968, Enoch Powell (a Conservative Member of Parliament) tried to defend the idea that immigrants were a threat to the British people in his "Rivers of blood" speech. It created a chasm in British society: part of the population was outraged by Powell's speech, whereas some found his dismissal from the government excessive.

- Margaret Thatcher, another Conservative, became Prime Minister in 1970. She was highly unpopular throughout her time in office and she resigned in 1979 after a dire period in British economy. In a speech she made in 1979, she accused strikers to be responsible for the fall of the economy. This speech was not well-received as the workers were striking to defend their rights.

2 Manipulation through totalitarian propaganda

- Other examples of speeches with negative impact are propaganda speeches. This kind of speech was satirised by George Orwell in *Animal Farm* (1945), an allegorical critic of the Soviet regime. As the novel opens, Major, a pig, persuades the animals to rebel against their owners and take control of the farm.

- In this "revolutionary" speech, Major makes a typical use of manipulative rhetoric tools. Pretending to put himself aside, he praises the audience in order to make them more apt to believe him. And once he has the animals' attention and confidence, he does not clearly state his ideas, but instead he deftly (*avec adresse*) leads them to formulate these in their own words, so they eventually believe Major's ideas are an expression of their wishes.

zoOm

"We should all be feminists"

In her TEDx talk, Chimamanda Ngozi Adichie focuses on feminism and her own relation to feminism. She uses examples from her personal experience in Nigeria and from her struggles after her move to America to show the impact of stereotypes and debunk them.

→ Watch Chimamanda Ngozi Adichie's talk: bit.ly/PbacAngTle_5a

6 Verbal jousting as an art form

En bref *If speeches and debates are part of history, these forms of verbal exchanges are also central to art. From trials becoming movie plots to novels revolving around the exchanges between characters, how can verbal exchanges become a form of art?*

I The theatricality of debates and speeches

1 Rhetoric in art

In language, rhetoric aims at convicing an audience through the use of figures of speech and other methods. A known example of rhetoric in art is Mark Antony's funeral oration in Shakespeare's play *Julius Caesar*. Although he does not directly denounce Caesar's murderers, he skilfully praises Caesar as a great leader and mourns his loss which he presents as detrimental for the Roman people. By doing so, he appeals to the crowd's emotions and turns people against Brutus and the conspirators. He therefore never explicitly states his opinion but indirectly leads his audience to agree with him.

2 Putting society on trial

- Award-winning courtroom dramas such as *12 Angry Men* (1957), *Mississippi Burning* (1988) and *Philadelphia* (1993) became popular thanks to their striking and compelling use of language.

INFO
A **courtroom drama** is a film or television genre in which the plot revolves around a real or fictional legal case and the justice system.

- *Philadelphia*'s main character, Andy, is a homosexual man living with AIDS. When Andy's bosses discover he is an AIDS patient, they fire him, which leads Andy to sue his former employers for discrimination. With popular actors such as Tom Hanks and Denzel Washington, as well as the courtroom setting, *Philadelphia* can be considered as a public trial of homophobic behaviours. The movie thus contributed to increase understanding and empathy for AIDS patient, who were at the time still often discriminated against.

II Debate as an art

1 Traditional and codified exchanges

- Verbal jousting is also a type of art with specific rules to follow. One can find an example of this in the British Parliament. Since the 1980s, the Queen's speech that opens parliamentary sessions was met by a jibe (*raillerie*) from Dennis Skinner, a Member of Parliament. This gradually became a tradition and the joke is now expected by politicians and the media every year.

One can also think of highly codified rap battles. The movie *8 Mile* (2003), starring rapper Eminem, contributed to elevate rap battles to the rank of art. A rap battle is an unprepared verbal fight in which rappers have to prove their talents. The movie shows how the main character first stuggles to win the battles and then how he goes on to defeat other rappers. What is also interesting in the movie is that real rappers were asked to participate in the filming and most of the rappers Eminem faces are Detroit-based artists.

2 Learning the art of debate

With so many examples of great public speakers, one must not forget that delivering speeches and participating in debates require practise. *The King's Speech* (2010) retraces King George VI's language therapy to overcome his stammer. This was of the highest importance as the King often needed to publicly address the British people.

Speeches and debates are however not reserved to kings. Debate clubs and debate teams are highly popular in the Anglosphere, especially in schools and universities. The movie *The Great Debaters* (2007) is an example of the importance of debate teams in the United States: the entire movie revolves around an African-American team and how they fight to be allowed to participate in debate competitions. They eventually face Harvard University, whose debate team is internationally recognised.

zoOm

Austen's witticisms

Joe Wright, *Pride and Prejudice*, 2005.

In Jane Austen's *Pride and Prejudice* (1813), a misunderstanding leads Elizabeth to treat Mr. Darcy with contempt. They only exchange witty and cutting remarks and often are on the verge of verbal fights. However, their respective wits lead them to fall in love with each other.

→ Watch the trailer of the movie: bit.ly/PbacAngTle_6a

MÉMO VISUEL

- **Avant-garde:** artists who experiment with their art forms and artworks in order to exceed traditional boundaries.
- **Censorship:** a ban on the publication or distribution of an artwork by a government.
- **Propaganda:** the use of the media and any communication system to convey a message aiming at influencing the population.
- **Rhetoric:** using figures of speech and emotions to persuade an audience.

Key ideas

Art forms and

Art and protest

Denouncing oppression

In the mid-1960s, the counterculture developed as a movement against the Vietnam War and the oppression of women in society.

Fighting for a fairer world

Exposing inequalities often entails denouncing the discrepancies between social classes in order to show poverty and social injustice.

debates of ideas

Art that sparks debate

Challenging taboos and myths
Through their work, artists can choose to reveal hidden truths about historical events and society, disputing established ideas.

Breaking the rules of art
In the 1960s, pop art rejected traditional art norms and forms to create artworks with everyday objects and themes.

The art of debate

The powerfulness of words
Great orators include John Fitzgerald Kennedy who rallied Americans to support the space program which eventually sent Neil Armstrong to the Moon.

Verbal jousting as an art form
Rap battles and debates have been elevated to the rank of art forms thanks to the mastery of words they require.

SE TESTER QUIZ

Vérifiez que vous avez bien compris les points clés des **fiches 1 à 6.**

1 Art and protest

→ FICHES 1 ET 2

1. Associez l'artiste au mouvement auquel il appartient.

a. George Orwell •	• anti-colonialist literature
b. Joan Baez •	• dystopian literature
c. Chinua Achebe •	• counterculture

2. Quel type d'art déplore le changement plutôt que de le promouvoir ?

☐ a. dystopian art
☐ b. reactionary art
☐ c. satire

2 Art that sparks debate

→ FICHES 3 ET 4

1. Quel roman a fait l'objet d'un procès pour obscénité ?

☐ a. J.D. Salinger's *The Catcher in the Rye* (1951)
☐ b. E.M. Forster's *Maurice* (1971)
☐ c. D.H. Lawrence's *Lady Chatterley's Lover* (1960)
☐ d. Evelyn Waugh's *Brideshead Revisited* (1945)

2. Vrai ou faux ? Cochez la case qui convient.

	V	F
a. Pop art denounces the consumer society.	☐	☐
b. Banksy criticises wealthy art collectors.	☐	☐
c. The YBAs favour traditional art forms.	☐	☐

3 The art of debate

→ FICHES 5 ET 6

1. Complétez le texte avec les mots qui conviennent.

The goal of speeches by great .... like MLK's "I Have a Dream" and JFK's "We choose to go to the Moon" is to gain .... They want to .... people to their cause. Those speeches .... people to rise up.

2. Retrouvez un synonyme pour chacun des mots ou groupe de mots suivants.

a. a speaker: an _ _ _ _ _ _
b. to mock: to _ _ _ _ _ _ _ _
c. a sarcastic remark: a _ _ _ _
d. a verbal argument: a _ _ _ _ _ _ _   _ _ _ _ _ _ _ _ _

S'ENTRAÎNER

4 Réviser le cours en 8 questions flash

1. What are the two opposing themes in war poetry?
2. How do Grayson Perry and William Hogarth use satire?
3. For what literary themes is Toni Morrison remembered for?
4. What was the goal of revisionist Westerns?
5. In what way does Imagist poetry differ from Romantic poetry?
6. What are the concepts invented by Orwell in 1984 to criticise totalitarianism?
7. What are some of the tools used in rhetoric?
8. What are the different forms of verbal exchanges?

5 Analyser une image

→ FICHE 23

Observez le tableau et répondez aux questions.

Document A

Wyndham Lewis (1882-1957) was a soldier during World War I. In 1917, he became a war artist and he was employed by the British and the Canadian governments.

Wyndham Lewis, *Officers and Signallers* (1918).

1. Spot the two main elements of the painting.

2. What can you notice about the depiction of the soldiers?

☐ a. They are drawn with geometrical forms.
☐ b. Their depiction is almost photo-realistic.
☐ c. They seem made of metal because of the colour used to paint them.

CONSEIL
Dans un document visuel, repérez d'abord :
- les différentes parties (*foreground*, *middle*, *background*) ;
- les couleurs ;
- les formes.

3. Use your answers to the previous questions to write a short paragraph describing and analysing the main elements in the painting. Focus on the colours and shapes to compare the depictions of the two main elements.

6 Analyser un texte d'idées

→ FICHE 22

Lisez le discours et répondez aux questions.

Document B

Winston Churchill gave his "We shall fight on the beaches" speech after the British army left Dunkirk during World War II. In his speech, he rallies spirits after the retreat which was successfully executed but was still a defeat for the British forces.

Even though large tracts of Europe and many old and famous States have fallen or may fall into the grip of the Gestapo and all the odious apparatus[1] of Nazi rule, we shall not flag or fail. We shall go on to the end. We shall fight in France, we shall fight on the seas and oceans, we shall fight with growing confidence and growing strength in the air, we shall defend our island, whatever the cost may be. We shall fight on the beaches, we shall fight on the landing grounds, we shall fight in the fields and in the streets, we shall fight in the hills; we shall never surrender, and if, which I do not for a moment believe, this island or a large part of it were subjugated and starving, then our Empire beyond the seas, armed and guarded by the British Fleet, would carry on the struggle, until, in God's good time, the New World, with all its power and might, steps forth to the rescue and the liberation of the old.

Extract from Winston Churchill's "We shall fight on the beaches" speech (June 4, 1940).

1. Apparatus: *mécanisme*

1. Lines 11 to 12: what does the "New World" steeping forth to the rescue of the "old (world)" refer to?

2. Spot the stylistic devices used in the speech and their intended effect:

Stylistic device	Intended effect
....	....
....	....
....	....
....	....

CONSEIL
N'oubliez pas d'analyser les spécificités propres à chaque type d'œuvres, en particulier pour les documents oratoires. Lisez le document dans votre tête pour repérer les procédés rhétoriques.

7 Analyser un poème

→ FICHE 20

Lisez les deux poèmes et répondez aux questions.

Document C

Richard Aldington wrote many poems denouncing the violence of the war.

Four days the earth was rent and torn
By bursting steel,
The houses fell about us;
Three nights we dared not sleep,
Sweating, and listening for the imminent crash
Which meant our death.

The fourth night every man,
Nerve-tortured, racked to exhaustion,
Slept, muttering[1] and twitching[2],
While the shells crashed overhead.

The fifth day there came a hush;
We left our holes
And looked above the wreckage of the earth
To where the white clouds moved in silent lines
Across the untroubled blue.

Richard Aldington, "Bombardment", *Images of War* (1919)

We sat together in the trench,
He on a lump of frozen earth
Blown in the night before,
I on an unexploded shell;
And smoked and talked, like exiles,
Of how pleasant London was,
Its women, restaurants, night clubs, theatres,
How at that very hour
The taxi cabs were taking folk to dine ...
Then we sat silent for a while
As a machine gun swept the parapet.

He said:
"I've been here on and off two years
And only seen one man killed."

"That's odd."

"The bullet hit him in the throat;
He fell in a heap[3] on the fire-step,
And called out 'My God! dead!'"

"Good Lord, how terrible!"

"Well, as to that, the nastiest job I've had
Was last year on this very front
Taking the discs at night from men
Who'd hung for six months on the wire
Just over there.
The worst of all was
They fell to pieces at a touch,
Thank God we couldn't see their faces;
They had gas helmets on ..."

I shivered:
"It's rather cold here, sir; suppose we move?"

Richard Aldington, "Trench Idyll", *War and Love* (1919)

1. muttering: *marmonnant* **2.** twitching: *tréssaillant* **3.** a heap: *un monceau*

1. Underline the words which belong to the lexical field of destruction.

2. Is the destruction depicted in the two poems only material? Justify your answer.

3. Apart from the lexical field of violence, how is the death of the soldiers alluded to?

CONSEIL
N'oubliez pas de repérer les différents **champs lexicaux**. Ils vous aideront à analyser les thèmes principaux du document.

OBJECTIF BAC

8 Synthèse de documents • *Art and protest*

Vous avez 3 heures 30 pour réaliser la synthèse et faire la traduction proposée. C'est à vous de vous organiser pour produire l'ensemble dans le temps imparti.

Les deux documents A (p. 25) et C (p. 27) que vous venez d'étudier et le document qui va suivre constituent l'ensemble de documents à analyser pour l'épreuve de synthèse concernant la thématique « Arts et débats d'idées » et plus particulièrement l'axe « Art et contestation ».

LE SUJET

Write a short commentary on the three documents (about 500 words): taking into account the specificities of each document, analyse how Aldington, Lewis and Heller use their respective art forms to denounce the consequences war has on soldiers.

Document D

Yossarian is the main character of Catch-22. *He is an American bombardier sent to Europe during World War II. Throughout his time in Europe, he attempts to find a way to be discharged from the military to go back to the United States.*

"Can't you ground someone who's crazy?"

"Oh, sure. I have to. There's a rule saying I have to ground anyone who's crazy."

"Then why don't you ground me? I'm crazy. Ask Clevinger."

"Clevinger? Where is Clevinger? You find Clevinger and I'll ask him."

"Then ask any of the others. They'll tell you how crazy I am."

"They're crazy."

"Then why don't you ground them?"

"Why don't they ask me to ground them?"

"Because they're crazy, that's why."

"Of course they're crazy," Doc Daneeka replied. "I just told you they're crazy, didn't I? And you can't let crazy people decide whether you're crazy or not, can you?"

Yossarian looked at him soberly and tried another approach.

"Is Orr crazy?"

"He sure is," Doc Daneeka said.

"Can you ground him?"

"I sure can. But first he has to ask me to. That's part of the rule."

"Then why doesn't he ask you to?"

"Because he's crazy," Doc Daneeka said. "He has to be crazy to keep flying combat missions after all the close calls he's had. Sure, I can ground Orr. But first he has to ask me to."

"That's all he has to do to be grounded?"

"That's all. Let him ask me."

"And then you can ground him?" Yossarian asked.

"No. Then I can't ground him."

"You mean there's a catch?"

"Sure there's a catch," Doc Daneeka replied. "Catch-22. Anyone who wants to get out of combat duty isn't really crazy."

There was only one catch and that was Catch-22, which specified that a concern for one's own safety in the face of dangers that were real and immediate was the process of a rational mind. Orr was crazy and could be grounded. All he had to do was ask; and as soon as he did, he would no longer be crazy and would have to fly more missions. Orr would be crazy to fly more missions and sane if he didn't, but if he was sane he had to fly them. If he flew them he was crazy and didn't have to; but if he didn't want to he was sane and had to. Yossarian was moved very deeply by the absolute simplicity of this clause of Catch-22 and let out a respectful whistle.

"That's some catch, that Catch-22," he observed.

"It's the best there is," Doc Daneeka agreed.

Yossarian saw it clearly in all its spinning reasonableness. There was an elliptical precision about its perfect pairs of parts that was graceful and shocking, like good modern art, and at times Yossarian wasn't quite sure that he saw it at all, just the way he was never quite sure about good modern art or about the flies Orr saw in Appleby's eyes. He had Orr's word to take for the flies in Appleby's eyes.

"Oh, they're there, all right," Orr had assured him about the flies in Appleby's eyes after Yossarian's first fight with Appleby in the officers' club, "although he probably doesn't even know it. That's why he can't see things as they really are."

"How come he doesn't know it?" inquired Yossarian.

"Because he's got flies in his eyes," Orr explained with exaggerated patience. "How can he see he's got flies in his eyes if he's got flies in his eyes?"

It made as much sense as anything else, and Yossarian was willing to give Orr the benefit of the doubt because Orr was from the wilderness outside New York City and knew so much more about wildlife than Yossarian did, and because Orr, unlike Yossarian's mother, father, sister, brother, aunt, uncle, in-law, teacher, spiritual leader, legislator, neighbor and newspaper, had never lied to him about anything crucial before. Yossarian had mulled his newfound knowledge about Appleby over in private for a day or two and then decided, as a good deed, to pass the word along to Appleby himself.

"Appleby, you've got flies in your eyes," he whispered helpfully as they passed by each other in the doorway of the parachute tent on the day of the weekly milk run to Parma.

"What?" Appleby responded sharply, thrown into confusion by the fact that Yossarian had spoken to him at all.

"You've got flies in your eyes," Yossarian repeated. "That's probably why you can't see them."

Joseph Heller, *Catch-22* (1961).

▶▶▶ LA FEUILLE DE ROUTE

→ Méthode détaillée de la synthèse dans le chapitre 4, p. 104

Étape 1 Analyser les termes du sujet

- *Consequences of the war*: impact de la guerre sur la population, sur les paysages et sur les soldats ; conséquences physiques et mentales.
- *Respective art forms*: utilisation des spécificités de chaque forme artistique pour arriver à un but commun.

Étape 2 Lire et analyser le corpus à la lumière de la problématique

- Problématique : In what ways is the gradual annihilation of the soldiers alluded to in the artistic depiction of the war?
- Repérer les différentes formes de destruction évoquées dans les documents.
- Commencer à réfléchir à une gradation des exemples pour construire le plan de façon logique.

Étape 3 Analyser et comparer l'apport de chaque document

	Depiction of soldiers	Allusions to death	Mimicking madness
Doc A: painting			
Doc B: poems			
Doc C: novel (extract)	• no first names, only family names or ranks (Doc Daneeka) • no precise depiction of the soldiers	• allusion to the "combat missions" flown by the pilots • madness directly linked to the constant threat of death	• reference to madness of the soldiers with the constant repetition of "crazy" • mental consequence of war on the soldiers • length of the novel which allows for a long circular passage on the Catch-22 • repetitions which mimick the circular reasoning of the conversation

Étape 4 Construire le plan de la synthèse

I. Depicting material damage
II. Dehumanising the soldiers
III. Intertwining death and madness

Étape 5 Rédiger la synthèse

→ CORRIGÉS p. 34

9 Traduction en français

→ *Méthode détaillée de la traduction dans le chapitre 6, p. 139*

LE SUJET

Traduisez les lignes 1 à 14 de l'extrait de *Catch-22*.

CONSEIL

Repérez les mots ou expressions récurrents. Ils doivent toujours être traduits de la même manière afin de ne pas perdre la cohérence du texte.

CORRIGÉS

SE TESTER QUIZ

1 Art and protest

1. a. dystopian literature • b. counterculture • c. anti-colonialist literature

2. b. Reactionary art is a reaction against change and not art promoting change. Reactionary artists would like things to go back to the way they were.

2 Art that sparks debate

1. c. When Penguin published the novel in 1960, they were attacked for publishing obscene material. However, they won the case.

2. a. Vrai. Pop art emerged in the 1950s when the consumerism was peaking in the UK and the US after World War II.
b. Vrai. With his anonymous sales and the shredding of *Girl with a Balloon*, Banksy confirmed his rejection of the wealthy art collection market.
c. Faux. The YBAs revolutionised British visual art in the late 1980s with new art forms and subjects.

> **CONSEIL**
> N'oubliez pas de justifier vos réponses par une référence précise. C'est ainsi que vous prouvez la validité de votre choix.

3 The art of debate

1. The goal of speeches by great orators like MLK's "I Have a Dream" and JFK's "We choose to go to the Moon" is to gain public support. They want to rally people to their cause. Those speeches inspire people to rise up.

2. a. a speaker: an orator • b. to mock: to satirise • c. a sarcastic remark: a jibe • d. a verbal argument: verbal jousting

S'ENTRAÎNER

4 Réviser le cours en 8 questions flash

1. Patriotic poetry which glorifies war as a patriotic duty and anti-war poetry which depicts the true brutality of war.

2. By using specificities from the upper-class (the manor in the countryside or the merchant being fitted for a suit), the artists satirise their subjects by depicting them in an exaggerated and ridiculous way.

3. She is remembered for her writings about slavery and the lives of Afro-Americans.

4. A revisionist Western takes up the traditional elements of the Western and reverses them to show how racist and misogynistic traditional Westerns can be.

5. Romantic poetry was about emotions and long contemplations whereas Imagist poetry is about everyday fleeting moments.

6. Big Brother is used to denounce the cult of personality and the telescreen is a metaphor for propaganda.

7. Skilful rhetoric is not about openly denouncing someone but on the contrary, it is about leading one's audience to denounce someone or something on their own thanks to praise and emotions.

8. The different forms of verbal exchanges are verbal jousting, rap battles and debates.

5 Analyser une image

1. Top left-hand corner: the **explosion**. Foreground: the **soldiers**.

2. a. The soldiers are drawn with geometrical forms and c. The soldiers seem made of metal because of the colour used to paint them.

3. The soldiers are dehumanised, **depicted** as lifeless metallic weapons. The geometrical organisation of their bodies **contrasts** with the depiction of the blast next to them. The blast is an uncontrolled mess of reddish mud that the soldiers protect themselves from. The dark red colour of the blast is a **reminder** of the blood spilled on the battle field. It once again **emphasises** the lifelessness of the soldiers: they are not the one bleeding but the earth is.

CONSEIL
Quand vous analysez une image, décrivez et expliquez d'abord chaque élément un par un, avant de les associer ou de les comparer.

6 Analyser un texte d'idées

1. The United States (the New World) coming to help European countries fighting Germany (the old word).

2.

Stylistic device	Intended effect
Polysyndeton = repetition of the conjunction "and" instead of commas ("large tracts of Europe *and* many old *and* famous States")	It changes the rhythm of the text and conveys the gravity of the situation of the soldiers in France.
Anaphora = repetitions at the beginning of sentences ("we shall fight")	It emphasises the most important part of the speech and make it easier to remember.
Alliteration = words starting with the same sound ("*f*lag or *f*ail" and "*s*ubjugated and *s*tarving")	It highlights word pairs to create urgency and emotional effect.

7 Analyser un poème

1. In the first poem: rent, torn, bursting, fell, crash, sweating, death, shells, crashed, exhaustion, wreckage.
In the second poem: unexploded shell, machine gun, killed, bullet, dead, fell to pieces, gas helmets.

2. No, the poem also depicts the **exhaustion of the soldiers**. The crash of the shells announces the soldiers' deaths (l. 6) and the physical consequences of the war are listed in the poem: "racked to exhaustion", "sweating".

3. In the first poem, the last stanza **casts doubt on the survival of the soldiers**. The "shells crashed overhead" and then the soldiers see "white clouds [...] across the untroubled blue". The clouds and the sky might be a euphemism for heaven, meaning the soldiers are dead. This idea is reinforced by the physical elevation of the soldiers: from a "hole", they see the "earth", then the clouds and the sky.
In the second poem, **dead bodies are clearly mentioned**: "men / Who'd hung for six months on the wire", and the description is highly visual: "They fell to pieces at a touch, / Thank God we couldn't see their faces". However, Aldington also alludes to death through the cold felt by the soldiers: they are sitting on a "lump of frozen earth" and then the speaker "shiver[s]". The poet here leads the reader to think of the coldness of bodies after death.

OBJECTIF BAC

8 Synthèse de documents • *Art and protest*

Les titres en couleur et les puces permettent de mettre en évidence la structure du corrigé mais ils ne figureraient pas sur une copie de bac.

Introduction

The documents under study are a painting by Wyndham Lewis, *Officers and Signallers*, two poems by Richard Aldington, and an excerpt from Joseph Heller's novel *Catch-22*. The three documents deal with the theme of war, and especially with the destruction caused by war, whether material, physical or mental. I shall therefore focus on the artistic depiction of the gradual annihilation of the soldiers in the documents.

CONSEIL
Assurez-vous que votre analyse prend bien en compte l'ensemble du corpus. Vérifiez que vous mentionnez toujours tous les documents dans chaque partie de votre synthèse.

I. Depicting material damage

■ First, destruction is central to the three documents. In the two poems, Aldington draws the attention of the reader to the **chaos surrounding the soldiers**. In "Bombardment", the shells are destroying everything around the men. In "Trench Idyll", the speaker is casually having a conversation while machine guns are being fired.

■ In Lewis' painting, this destruction incurred by war is visible in the right-hand top corner of the painting with the blast from the explosion. The earth is being torn under the soldiers' feet. However, the soldiers do not seem to be affected by the exploding shell: they are depicted walking, moving on even though their lives are in danger. With those visual elements, the viewer necessarily **faces the destruction incurred by war**. Lewis therefore made the war visible for civilians who were not on the front.

■ In the extract from *Catch-22*, the destruction is only alluded to but still present. Both Yossarian and the doctor mention the combat missions in which the soldiers drop bombs, and how dangerous those missions are through Orr's many "close-calls". Just as in the poems and the painting, chaos and destruction surround the men but they do not seem affected. By alluding to death and not mentioning it directly, the reader is led to understand that the **threat of death is always looming**.

II. Dehumanising the soldiers

■ Then, in Heller's novel, the characters are **defined by their last names and their ranks**. Their first names are rarely used, as the military fashion dictates. Their identities are limited to their roles. The personalities of the soldiers are therefore erased, they become disposable fighters that can be replaced easily, just as weapons would be. By not giving names, the reader cannot easily relate with the soldiers: he is led by the author to see them as soldiers only.

■ Wyndham Lewis was a Vorticist painter, and the Vorticist influence can be seen in the depiction of the soldiers: their bodies are drawn with harsh straight lines. The colours used to paint the five men also make their bodies look like they are made of metal. **The soldiers resemble weapons** more than human beings. In addition, each one of them is drawn in an identitical fashion, as though they had been mass produced with the same mold. The technique used by the painter forces the reader to confront the utility and not the personality of the soldiers.

■ In Aldington's poems, the soldiers remain unidentified as well. They are only referred to thanks to personal pronouns "we", "he", and "I". There is therefore a contrast between the **anonymity of the soldiers** and the intimate knowledge the reader has about the characters' fear of dying. The poetic form also allows Aldington to convey the violence of the war without allowing the reader to identify with the soldiers. There is thus a discrepancy between the intimacy conveyed by the poem and its short nature: the reader is only a spectator of the scene.

> **CONSEIL**
> Pour chaque idée, n'oubliez pas d'apporter une **citation** ou un **exemple** tiré des documents et de l'analyser pour ensuite expliquer l'effet produit et le but de l'artiste.

III. Intertwining death and madness

■ The dehumanisation process of the soldiers is complete as the documents allude to death and madness. In the painting, the colours are chosen to allude to death: the blast is reddish brown, just as blood. The earth takes on the colour of flesh which is burst open. The painter has here replaced the depiction of dying bodies by showing the destruction of **the earth which becomes the victim of war**.

■ In "Bombardment", the soldiers only sleep on the fourth day, but it is a restless and "nerve-tortured" sleep. They are affected by sleep deprivation and cannot think straight anymore. The restlessness of the soldiers and the length of the day are mirrored in the structure of the poem: each stanza is composed of one sentence only. The **deterioration of the thinking process** can also be found in "Trench Idyll": the conversation about dead bodies is casual and the soldiers have become insensitive to the destruction around them. The reader is also forced to become insensitive to dead bodies as well: Aldington's poem is not an epic poem glorifying the sacrifices of soldiers but a raw depiction of soldiers being killed.

■ In Heller's extract, physical death is not the issue. However, the **circular reasoning** of the two characters is used by the author to mirror the developing madness of the soldiers. The circularity of the reasoning is conveyed by the repetitive nature of the conversation between Yossarian and Doc Daneeka which is developed in the chapter. The absurdity of war and the fear of death has made the soldiers insane as they contemplate their helplessness. They may not die on the front, but the war has made them crazy.

Conclusion

To conclude, the documents first focus on material destruction, the immediate consequence of the war and of the bombardments, with references to weapons and artillery. Then, the soldiers lose their personality and uniqueness through a dehumanising process that turns them into war machines: they do not have names and are not identifiable. Lastly, the destruction culminates in the alienation and death of the soldiers which are alluded to by a circular mode of writing.

9 Traduction en français

Yossarian le regarda calmement et tenta une nouvelle approche.
« Est-ce qu'Orr est fou ?
– Bien sûr, répondit Doc Daneeka.
– Est-ce que vous pouvez le bloquer au sol ?
– Bien sûr. Mais il doit me demander d'abord. C'est la règle.
– Pourquoi est-ce qu'il ne vous le demande pas alors ?
– Parce qu'il est fou, répondit Doc Daneeka. Il doit être fou pour continuer à effectuer des vols de combat après l'avoir échappé belle / échappé de justesse tant de fois. Bien sûr que je peux bloquer Orr au sol. Mais il doit me demander d'abord.
– C'est tout ce qu'il a à faire pour être bloqué au sol ?
– C'est tout. Il doit me demander.
– Et vous pourrez le bloquer au sol ? demanda Yossarian.
– Non. Je ne pourrai pas le bloquer au sol.
– Vous voulez dire qu'il y a un piège / une entourloupe ?
– Bien sûr qu'il y a un piège / une entourloupe, répondit Doc Daneeka. Le piège / l'entourloupe 22. Tous ceux qui veulent être déchargés de leurs missions de combat ne sont pas vraiment fous. »

2 Expression and construction of the self

If art and history are crucial in understanding a given culture, taking a closer look at how individuals build themsleves within that cultural context may help to better understand it.

7 Emotions in art

En bref *Emotions are a set of complex feelings ranging from positive ones such as joy or love, to more negative ones like grief, or despair. Throughout history, artists have been concerned with expressing emotions and representing them in their work. How have art and artistic movements represented emotions?*

I Art as a medium to express emotions

1 Representing diverse emotions

- Human emotions have long constituted the very material of art and they can be expressed no matter the artistic medium. In Shakespeare's *Hamlet* (c. 1604), Ophelia sings of her despair before committing suicide by drowing. In *Ophelia* (1851), Pre-Raphaelite painter John Everett Millais depicts a moving portrait of Ophelia's corpse floating in water among flowers.

INFO
The **Pre-Raphaelite** brotherhood was a society of young artists opposed to Raphael's classical ideals of beauty (namely the representation of an idealized human form).

- Artists have often used their own emotions in the making of their work. For example, in "In Memoriam A.H.H." (1850), Lord Alfred Tennyson expresses his own grief and laments over the death of his closest friend. However, beyond the mere expression of the poet's feelings, this elegiac poem takes on a more universal meaning and delves into the nature of sorrow.

- An emotion may serve as the very subject matter of an artistic piece. In Pharrell Williams's hit pop song "Happy" (2013), the singer uses both music and lyrics to describe happiness itself.

2 Expressing the intensity of feelings

- One of the purposes of art is the expression of emotions, to different degrees. Love is one of the most intense of feelings and love song is an extremely well-represented genre in pop music. Song expresses emotions through verbal means and through the music itself. While The Beatles expressed the lighter side of love in "All You Need is Love" (1967), contemporary singers such as Adele focus on heartbreak in songs like "Rolling in the Deep" (2011).

- Art may be used to explore the human condition and deal with darker and powerful emotions. In Edward Albee's play, *Who's Afraid of Virginia Woolf?* (1962), the disturbing depiction of the protagonists' emotional struggle following the death of their child pervades (*imprègne*) the work although it is not revealed up until the end.

II Emotions as a source for artistic movements

Self-expression has been central to the creation of several artistic movements highlighting emotions in codified forms.

1 Romanticism and the "overflow of feelings"

- British Romanticism began as a response to the Industrial Revolution, celebrating personal feeling and rejecting social conventions. Early Romantic poets such as William Wordsworth ("I Wandered Lonely as a Cloud", 1802) emphasized the importance of nature and solitude. Later Romantics, such as Lord Byron (*Don Juan,* 1819; *Childe Harold's Pilgrimage,* 1818), were more politicized and advocated personal freedom.
- The Romantic movement continues on, for instance in movies like Jane Campion's *Bright Star* (2009) in which she portrays John Keats ("Ode to a Nightingale", 1819), whose work and life embodied the ideals of Romanticism.

2 Transcendentalism: the self and the universe

- Transcendentalism is an American cultural movement that stemmed from English Romanticism in the late 19th century. It focused on emotions as well as senses, creativity and individualism. Its most famous proponents, Henry David Thoreau and Ralph Waldo Emerson believed that each individual was part of infinite nature.
- Walt Whitman's *Leaves of Grass* (1855-1891) took up aspects of Transcendentalist ideas, such as the link between macrocosm and microcosm, and lent it poetic form. However, Whitman's emphasis on sexuality led him to create an artform that was his own, and break away from pure transcendentalism.

zoOm

Melancholia

- During the Renaissance, it was believed that a person's character was determined by the balance of humours (fluids) in their bodies.
- The imbalance of humours was thought to cause a disturbed personality. Melancholia (excessive sadness) was then thought to be the result of the excess of black bile.

→ Listen to this BBC programme on the theory of humours: bit.ly/PbacAngTle_7a

Melancholy young man, oil on canvas, unknown artist, c. 1584-c. 1588.

8 Emotional responses to art

En bref *Intentional or not, art provokes emotional responses, which have often been argued to constitute its very purpose. How can art be used in order to tap into the feelings of an audience?*

I Art as an emotional experience

1 The purification of emotions

- The first theory of the emotional experience of art is to be found in Aristotle's *Poetics* (c. 335 BC). The philosopher coined the term *catharsis* to refer to the purging of one's emotions through art. This was first used to discuss tragedy, which was then believed to purge the audience of their own negative feelings by witnessing the violent actions and feelings displayed onstage.

- The cinema also plays this role today. In *Django Unchained* (2013), director Quentin Tarentino rewrites the history of slavery and has his hero seek revenge on white slave owners. Catharsis here is twofold – as an individual, the viewer is made to feel for the character and as a citizen, he is made to take pleasure in seeing the wrongs of history finally righted (*corrigés*) onscreen.

2 Emotions, by all means?

- Art may represent a distorted reality in order to have a strong impact on the audience. Francis Bacon, inspired by **expressionism**, painted the classical figure of the Pope as a nightmarish vision, in his *Study after Velasquez's Pope Innocent X* (1953), leading the viewer to experience horror in its rawest (*la plus crue*) form.

> **INFO**
> **Expressionism**, which originated in Germany in the early 20th century, emphasizes subjective representations aiming for strong emotional responses.

- American painter Jackson Pollock was famous for his "drip technique" – throwing paint at the canvas. Creating a strong emotional response despite not using a realistic subject matter, his art was labelled abstract expressionism. One of his most famous paintings, *Convergence* (1952), in spite of being difficult to decipher (*déchiffrer*), aims at having the audience feel for themselves the freedom the artist experienced while creating this piece.

II Using emotions for political purposes

1 Raising political awareness

- Emotions may be mustered to raise awareness. For instance, conscious hip hop artists from the 1980s and 1990s such as Run-DMC voiced emotions to convey strong, and effective political messages.

- Most famously, Coolio expressed anger in *Gangsta's Paradise* (1995) to expose the plight *(situation critique)* of black people in America's poorest neighbourhoods at the end of the 20th century.
- Banksy's famous murals, such as *I remember when all this was trees* (2010), serve the same purpose. Leaving his art in unexpected places leads people who wouldn't ordinarily go to a museum to be influenced by his thought-provoking art. Surprise becomes an emotion as the artist uses it to convey oriented messages to an audience of passersby.

2 | Persuasion and manipulation

- Using emotions to persuade an audience is one of the most important characteristics of the art of **rhetoric**. President J.F. Kennedy's command of language allowed him to be particularly persuasive in speeches such as his *Inaugural Address* (1961) in which his use of repetitions, juxtapositions and biblical quotes helped convey his message of peace.

INFO
Rhetoric is the art or skill of influencing people through effective use of language in any given situation.
→ FICHE 6

- George Orwell exposes the dangers inherent to rhetoric in *1984* (1949) where a new language, Newspeak, is invented and expunged of meaning in order to control the population's thoughts and feelings. Syme, a character working on the newest version of the Newspeak dictionary, marvels at "the destruction of words". Using several examples (*ungood* instead of *bad*), Syme demonstrates how the government aims at limiting people's experience by limiting the capacities of language.

zoOm

I remember when all of this was trees

In 2010, British Artist Banksy chose a dilapidated plant in Detroit to paint one of his famous murals. He uses the surroundings to produce a work of art containing a simple message that will lead the viewer to both feel and reflect upon his own time.

→ Discover more about Banksy: bit.ly/PbacAngTle_8a

Banksy, *I remember when all this was trees*. Aerosol on cinder-block wall, 2010, Detroit.

9 Exploring the self through art

En bref *When interviewed on television, performance artist Leigh Bowery stated that he saw himself as a blank canvas that had to be painted upon. Many artists have used their own body or image in the making of their art. In what way can this "staging" of the self be understood both as a reflection on individuality and art?*

I The self as subject and object of art

Self-representation may be perceived as egotism. However, artists often use their body or image to create art that explores the very notion of the self.

1 The self as a canvas

- English painter and photographer David Hockney has produced over three hundred drawn or photographic self-portraits. In these works, the artist studies himself at different stages of his life, offering the viewer an intellectual reflection on the passage of time.
- The work of American photographer Cindy Sherman essentially consists in series of close-ups of herself impersonating a wide range of different characters. In her landmark series, *Untitled Film Stills* (1977-1980), Cindy Sherman deconstructs the very notion of the self by disappearing into a multiplicity of female characters.

2 Altering the ego

- Many artists have created alter egos which serve as an exploration of the artist's self. Most famously, in *The Picture of Dorian Gray* (1891) Lord Henry Wotton is a witty and provocative character based on Oscar Wilde himself, who embodies **dandyism** throughout the novel. Fictional doubles of Oscar Wilde are also to be found throughout his work – in both his plays and his short stories.

> **INFO**
> **Dandyism** is the term used to describe the style of 19th century fashionable gentlemen and the artistic movement emphasizing the sophistication that stemmed from it.

- English artist Grayson Perry uses cross-dressing throughout his work, dressing up to his female alter ego, Claire, in series of photographs and **performances**. Through transvestism, the artist distorts and explores his own image hence questioning the traditional representation of a gendered self.

> **INFO**
> **Performance art** is an art form based on presenting a situation to an audience. It often involves the presence of the artist, and sometimes even his or her own body.

II Investigating one's art

Autobiography and self-portraiture may also be used in order to further understand art itself.

1 Autobiographical enquiries

- In *One Writer's Beginnings* (1984), novelist Eudora Welty discusses her childhood in the American South to understand the bond between her upbringing and her later career as a writer. She emphasizes how her early relationship with her father and taste for reading shaped her desire to become a writer.
- George Orwell's approach is more intellectual. In his essay, *Why I Write* (1946), he explains how political events, namely the Spanish War led him to become a writer. This "political purpose" to writing is one of the four great motives Orwell lists in this work.

2 Using a fictional double to explore art

- Fictional doubles may serve as an investigation into the making of an artist. In *A Portrait of the Artist as a Young Man* (1916), James Joyce experiments with new techniques and tells his own story as he is growing to become a major writer. Both his alter ego, Dedalus, and the literary technique he uses, free indirect speech, took on an even more refined form in his masterpiece, *Ulysses* (1922).
- Woody Allen's early work often features a neurotic New Yorker in which he portrays himself. In *Deconstructing Harry* (1997), the main character's life is told from multiple perspectives underlining the link between an artist and his work – his love life finds its way into his writings which in turn impact his "real life".

zoom

Girls

- The series *Girls* (2012-2017) tells the story of four young women striving to get on with their lives in a somewhat hostile city.
- The main character, Hannah Horvath, is played by actress and director Lena Dunham who grew to become the "voice of a generation".

→ Watch the trailer of season 1: bit.ly/PbacAngTle_9a

Lena Dunham, *Girls*, Season 2.
Television show promotional poster.

10 History in self-making

En bref *Through the analysis of archives, or findings from archeology, experts are able to write history as we know it today. However, some people have used their own stories in order to participate in writing history. How do personal narratives help shape collective history?*

I Writing oneself into history

1 Actors and witnesses

- In his *Memoirs of the Second World War* (1948-1953), Winston Churchill discusses the war from his point of view. This now famous historical work has been widely read and studied, hence shaping the way we see and understand World War II today. However, some commentators have accused Churchill of "reconstructing the story" for personal and political reasons.
- In *The Autobiography of Benjamin Franklin* (1793), Benjamin Franklin gives an account of his life in the late 18th century and of the events that led to the Declaration of Independence. Franklin emphasizes how hard he worked to succeed, participating in the creation of the myth of the self-made man which has become central in American culture.

2 Using oneself in art to remember and to commemorate

- Artists such as Vivian Maier chose to bear witness to their era by capturing it through photography. However, she added self-portraits to her photographs of New York in the 1950s in which her image becomes one with the city around her.
- Louis MacNeice's poems interweave the poet's personal life and failures with political concerns about his time in *The Burning Perch* (1963); emphasizing for instance the fear of the atomic bomb. MacNeice and other poets from the 1930s such as Auden and Spender, are sometimes referred to as "the Auden group", whose works were personal, political, and critical of their time.

II Challenging history

1 Reappropriating history

- Twenty years before the abolition of slavery, Frederick Douglass, an academic and former slave, published *A Narrative of the Life of Frederick Douglass* (1845) an account of his own experience of being an enslaved person. This landmark narrative fueled the abolitionist movement by making a slave narrative public.

INFO
Slave narratives constitute a literary genre which features autobiographical accounts of enslaved people.

■ In *You Don't Have to Say You Love Me* (2017), Sherman Alexie reflects upon his own upbringing in a Native American reservation. By focusing on his mother's life and character, he participates in telling the stories of Native American people today.

■ In the non-fiction story *I Love Dick (1997)*, Chris Kraus uses her own experience of creating art to bring the work of female artists, which had gone unnoticed because of their gender, to the forefront.

2 | Subverting history

■ Some artists have used their medium to mock historical symbols and criticize the actions of their governments. In 1969, Jimmy Hendrix sang a version of the Star-Spangled Banner that subverted the meaning of the anthem to criticize the ongoing Vietnam War.

■ In *Bloody Sunday* (2002), director Paul Greengrass chose to change the focus of how the Bloody Sunday events are seen by showing them through the eyes of Ivan Cooper, a politician and civil rights activist whose role was central in the events leading to the massacre. → ANNEXES History is thus re-told not by the English, but from the point of view of the Irish who were oppressed.

INFO
The **Bloody Sunday Massacre** (1972) took place in Derry, Northern Ireland during a civil rights march. thirty unarmed civilians were killed by British troops.

zoOm

The Autobiography of Benjamin Franklin

Benjamin Franklin's life was remarkable: he was a well-travelled scientist, writer and politician. His ground-breaking autobiography exemplifies the hybridity of the genre, being both a major work of literature and a historical record.

→ Read the beginning of Franklin's autobiography: bit.ly/PbacAngTle_10a

Joseph Siffred Duplessis, *Portrait of Benjamin Franklin*, 1785.

11 Growing up in the Anglo-Saxon world

En bref *Childhood, adolescence, and adulthood are three moments that mark the passage of time in a person's life. However, these moments of life are greatly shaped by the culture in which the individual grows up. What have art and history taught us about growing up in the English-speaking world?*

I Becoming an adult: a cultural challenge

1 The trials of adolescence

■ The concept of adolescence is a modern one: prior to social changes brought about at the turn of the 19th century (Child Labour laws and universal education), children worked early on and were considered adults in their teens. 20th and 21st century art has endeavoured to tackle this new stage of human development during which major physical and psychological changes occur. In Sylvia Plath's *The Bell Jar* (1963) the heroine, epitomising (*est l'emblème de*) teenage years in the 20th century, fails to fit in and find her *self* in spite of her attempts to do so.

■ Critically acclaimed British TV show *Skins* (2007-2013) portrayed the sense of loss common to a generation of **millennials** growing up in the early 21st century. Focusing on one character at a time, the series expanded on the protagonists' experimenting with drug taking and sexuality to reflect upon the experience of adolescence as a difficult moment of passage.

> **INFO**
> **Millennials** refers to the generation of people born between the early 1980s and the mid 2000s thus coming of age during the growth of the Internet.

2 Meeting with the other to become oneself

■ Life experiences also help shape the individual self of an adult for better or for worse. Travel can constitute an important experience during which the individual learns from the discovery of a different culture. In Britain in the 17th and 18th century, the Grand Tour → FICHE 13 was a part of the education of young men from the gentry. Young men who had come of age were sent to Europe to learn about culture and the arts.

■ Some encounters may be significant in a person's life. Meeting with a mentor or a spiritual guide sometimes helps the individual discover themselves. In *Million Dollar Baby* (2004), a young woman decides to take up boxing and forms a strong relationship with her boxing trainer, which will eventually end up in her downfall.

II Growing up outside of the norms of society

1 Growing up the hard way

- Exterior events sometimes force the individual to find the means to survive. World War II left thousands of children orphaned. While childhood usually is a stage of life in which the individual is protected by his parents, these children had to survive and learn how to live in horrific socio-economic conditions.

- In his famous novel *Lord of the Flies* (1954), William Golding depicts a dystopian fictional world in which young boys stranded on a desert island attempt and fail to establish law and order among themselves, leading to atrocities. In the absence of adults the boys learn about human nature without civilisation, only to revert back to being children when rescued, crying.

2 Emancipation or confrontation with society

- Emancipating may entail the building of one's self in spite of or against social norms. Up until the early 20th century, women were considered as children. During World War II, figures such as Rosie the Riveter, a fictional character used in several propaganda posters (including J. Howard Miller's "*We Can Do It*", 1943), were used to incite women to take part in the war effort. Rosie later became an American icon for the feminist movement.

- In *Crossing the River* (1993) Caryl Phillips discusses the African diaspora by giving a voice to fictional characters who have had to face racial prejudice throughout their lives. Spanning over two centuries, the novel focuses on how those characters eventually overcome this prejudice and become emancipated.

zoOm

Growing up in the Second World War

The Blitz refers to a German bombing campaign which took place in 1940-41. Its effects were devastating for Britain. In that time period, an entire generation of children were evacuated and grew up far from their parents. The Imperial War Museum in London has exhibited pictures taken during that period.

→ Look at the pictures on the IWM website: bit.ly/PbacAngTle_11a

A policeman helps young evacuees and the nun escorting them at a London station on 18 May 1940. Imperial War Museum, © IWM (LN 6194).

12 Are education novels educational?

En bref *Education novels are a well-established literary genre in English literature which specifically deal with a character's evolution throughout their life. How does the depiction of education in novels serve an educational purpose?*

I Depicting education

1 Capturing the process of coming of age

- ***Bildungsromans*** portray the coming of age of their protagonists. *The History of Tom Jones, a Foundling,* by Henry Fielding (1749), can be considered as a **prototypical education novel**. The protagonist's story is told from his early childhood to adulthood and focuses on both the mystery of his origins and his romantic relationship with a young woman.

- J.K. Rowling's *Harry Potter* (1997-2007) constitutes a **contemporary instance of the coming of age story**. Hogwarts is used as a setting from Rowling's imaginary wizarding world and mirrors the context in which British youngsters grow up today.

2 In quest of the self

- The character's evolution in education novels is often used as a way to **explore human nature and the passage of time**. In *The Mill on the Floss* by George Elliot (1860), the stories of two siblings are recounted over fifteen years, emphasizing the differences in their trajectories. Their **psychological and intellectual development** is touched on as their differing life choices enfold.

> **INFO**
> **George Elliot** was a major 18th century novelist. Her work chiefly focuses on the development of young characters from the Midlands.

- In Harper Lee's *To Kill a Mockingbird* (1960), the two protagonists witness their father, a lawyer, defending a black man accused of rape. The atrocities surrounding this event participates in their **moral development**.

II Educating the reader

1 The moral undertones of education novels

- The use of symbols is one of the literary devices used for an educational purpose. Daniel Defoe's *Roxana, The Fortunate Mistress* (1724) is a first person narrative in which a prostitute tells about how she came to sell her body. The novel focuses on her moral decay, brought about by society, feeding into **the motif of the fallen woman**.

■ *Oliver Twist* (1837), by Charles Dickens is the story of an orphan who has to grow up in the streets of a drab (*morne*), industrial London. Throughout the novel, Dickens makes extensive use of symbols, endowing some of the characters with biblical characteristics leading the reader to understand which characters are good and which are evil. Those symbols are often used to build upon the social commentary that is present throughout the novel.

2 | Addressing the reader: for what purpose?

■ Narratorial comments are often used in education novels to explicitly make a moral comment in order to guide the reader. In Charlotte Brontë's *Jane Eyre* (1847), the narrator addresses the reader directly in the famous line: "Reader, I married him". By involving the reader in the novel, Brontë contributes to drawing them into the heroine's moral dilemmas.

■ Through a complex set of authorial comments and weaving of the plot, Jane Austen's *Sense and Sensibility* (1811) makes great use of **didacticism** and takes a moral stance against sensibility, a fashion of the late 18th century which involved overblown sensitivity and taste for the picturesque (*pittoresque*). Marianne, a character who embodies sensibility ends up realising that she was wrong in being driven only by her feelings and eventually decides to become more sensible.

> **INFO**
> **Didacticism** is a type of literature whose aim is to educate and inform the reader in political, or often moral matters.

zoOm

Boyhood

■ *Boyhood* (2014) uses all the ressources of cinema to depict the main character's coming of age, as the director shot the film over a period of twelve years.

■ By witnessing the actual growth of the characters onscreen, the viewer is forced to reflect upon the coming of age process and the passage of time.

→ Watch the trailer of *Boyhood*: bit.ly/PbacAngTle_12a

Boyhood, Film poster. Richard Linklater, 2014.

MÉMO VISUEL

- **The self:** a set of personal psychological characteristics which make someone unique. Yet, the self evolves as time passes and as the individual learns from experience.
- **An alter ego:** literally "second I", also known as "double". In art and literature, it refers to a fictional being that represents a deformed mirror image of the author which can be used as an exploration of the self.
- **History** vs. **story:** while history refers to the record of important events, stories are personal narratives, be they fictional or non-fictional.

Key ideas

Expression and construction

The expression of emotions

Emotions in art

Art and emotions are entwined (*intriqués*). Emotions have been at the very core of artistic movements such as Romanticism or Transcendentalism.

Emotional responses to art

Art provokes positive and negative feelings in the people who experience it. Artists can manipulate their audience, through their feelings.

Exploring the self through art

Some artists have chosen self-representation as a means of expression. By staging their selves, these artists explore both themselves and their artform.

Staging the self

History in self-making

Historical figures, artists and ordinary people have contributed to writing history through personal narratives, memoirs and autobiographies.

of the self

Initiation and learning

Growing up in the Anglo-Saxon world

The process of growing up is one that is culturally bound. However, these boundaries or norms have been challenged leading to growth in both individuals and humanity.

Are education novels educational?

The education novel, which is widely represented in Anglo-Saxon literature, focuses on a protagonist whose moral and psychological evolution is narrated as they grow up.

SE TESTER QUIZ

Vérifiez que vous avez bien compris les points clés des **fiches 7 à 12.**

1 The expression of emotions

→ FICHES 7 ET 8

1. Associez chaque œuvre à son mouvement artistique.

a. *Convergence* •	• Transcendentalism
b. *Leaves of Grass* •	• Romanticism
c. "Ode to a Nightingale" •	• Abstract Expressionism

2. Vrai ou faux ? Cochez la case qui convient.

	V	F
a. Lord Alfred Tennyson expressed his own emotions in "In Memoriam A.H.H.".	☐	☐
b. Romantics were only concerned with representing emotion.	☐	☐
c. Catharsis is a term that initially referred to tragedy.	☐	☐
d. In *1984*, Newspeak is a made-up language which emphasizes emotion.	☐	☐

2 Staging the self

→ FICHES 9 ET 10

1. Trouvez un synonyme pour chacun des mots ou groupe de mots suivants.

a. a picture that represents the artist (n) : a _ _ _ _ - _ _ _ _ _ _ _ _ _ _ _

b. individuality (n) : the _ _ _ _

c. an autobiography written by an enslaved person (n) : a _ _ _ _ _ _ _ _ _ _ _ _ _ _ _ _ _ _

d. to be the spectator of an event (v) : to _ _ _ _ _ _ _ _ _

2. Cochez la ou les propositions qui conviennent.

Which artists have created alter egos in their work?

☐ a. Eudora Welty ☐ b. Grayson Perry ☐ c. George Orwell

3 Initiation and learning

→ FICHES 11 ET 12

1. Vrai ou faux ? Cochez la case qui convient.

	V	F
a. In the 17th and 18th century, all young men went on the Grand Tour.	☐	☐
b. During the Blitz, children had to survive in horrific conditions.	☐	☐
c. In *Crossing the River*, the characters become emancipated.	☐	☐

2. Complétez le texte ci-dessous avec les mots qui conviennent.

Many artists have tried to tackle the .... process, but the one genre that did it most famously was the .... novel, or .... Those novels often focus on a protagonist's mental, psychological and .... development and help the reader understand .... nature.

S'ENTRAÎNER

4 Réviser le cours en 8 questions flash

1. What did the romantics emphasize in their work?
2. Why was Run-DMC's rap different from rap songs from their era?
3. What is the difference between Cindy Sherman's and David Hockney's self-portraits?
4. What movement is represented in *The Picture of Dorian Gray*?
5. What problem was raised by Churchill's memoirs?
6. What is the link between Franklin's autobiography and American culture?
7. What issue did Chris Kraus raise in *I love Dick*?
8. What literary devices can often be found in education novels?

5 Analyser un poème

→ FICHE 20

Lisez le poème au moins deux fois et répondez aux questions.

Document A

"Song of Myself" was the first poem in Leaves of Grass. *In sections 1 and 24 of the poem, Whitman famously introduces both himself and his poetry to the reader.*

1
I celebrate myself, and sing myself,
And what I assume you shall assume,
For every atom belonging to me as good belongs to you.

I loafe[1] and invite my soul,
I lean and loafe at my ease observing a spear of summer grass.

My tongue, every atom of my blood, form'd from this soil[2], this air,
Born here of parents born here from parents the same, and their parents the same,
I, now thirty-seven years old in perfect health begin,
Hoping to cease not till death.

Creeds[3] and schools in abeyance[4],
Retiring back a while sufficed at what they are, but never forgotten,
I harbor[5] for good or bad, I permit to speak at every hazard,
Nature without check with original energy.

24
Walt Whitman, a kosmos, of Manhattan the son
Turbulent, fleshy, sensual, eating, drinking and breeding[6],

No sentimentalist, no stander above men and women or apart from them
No more modest than immodest. (...)

Whoever degrades another degrades me,
And whatever is done or said returns at last to me. (...)

I speak the password primeval[7], I give the sign of democracy,
By God! I will accept nothing which all cannot have their counterpart of
 on the same terms.

Through me many long dumb voices,
Voices of the interminable generations of prisoners and slaves,
Voices of the diseas'd and despairing and of thieves and dwarfs,
Voices of cycles of preparation and accretion
And of the threads that connect the stars, and of wombs[8] and of the
 father-stuff,
And of the rights of them the others are down upon,
Of the deformed, trivial, flat, foolish, despised
Fog in the air, beetles rolling balls of dung
Through me forbidden voices,
Voices of sexes and lust, voices veil'd and I remove the veil,
Voices indecent by me clarified and transfigur'd.

I do not press my fingers across my mouth,
I keep as delicate around the bowels[9] as around the head and heart,
Copulation is no more rank to me than death is.

I believe in the flesh and the appetites,
Seeing, feeling, are miracles, and each part and tag of me is a miracle.

Walt Whitman, "Song of Myself", *Leaves of Grass* (1955), sections 1 et 24.

1. loafe: *flemmarder* 2. soil: *la terre* 3. creeds: *croyances* 4. abeyance: *suspension*
5. harbor: *héberger* 6. breeding: *ici, avoir des relations sexuelles*
7. I speak the password primeval: here, Whitman intuits that he holds the secrets of the past
8. wombs: *uterus* 9. bowels: *intestins*

1. Complete the chart to match at least one line of the text with a corresponding adjective.

	Quotes / examples
Provocative	
Empathetic	
All-encompassing	

2. Who is the poem addressed to?

☐ **a.** The reader ☐ **b.** America ☐ **c.** The universe

3. How are the two elements of the poem's title reflected in the structure, rhythm and literary devices used in the poem?

HELP
- Why is the structure of the poem original?
- Spot repeated words and say what effect they have.
- Focus on the first stanza of each section: how is the speaker's self represented?

6 Analyser une image

→ FICHE 23

Regardez l'image et répondez aux questions.

Document B

Leigh Bowery was a performance artist and fashion designer from the 1980s. His work was influential in the gay night scene from that era.

Leigh Bowery, c1983. Photograph by Sheila Rock. Exhibited at RMIT Gallery as a part of the *Look At Me: Leigh Bowery* exhibition.

1. Analyze the title of the exhibition. How does the picture relate to it?

2. With a pencil, circle some elements in the picture:

a. Draw a square ☐ around items that are usually associated with femininity

b. Draw a circle ◯ around items that are usually associated with masculinity.

c. What does it tell us about the representation of gender in this work?

3. Analyze the compostion and colours of the picture. What do they convey?

HELP
- Can you spot contrasts?
- Is the picture evocative of a culture you know about?

OBJECTIF BAC

7 Synthèse de documents • *Expression et construction de soi*

Vous avez 3 heures 30 pour réaliser la synthèse et faire la traduction proposée. C'est à vous de vous organiser pour produire l'ensemble dans le temps imparti.

Les deux documents A et B que vous venez d'étudier et le document (C) qui va suivre constituent l'ensemble de documents à analyser pour l'épreuve de synthèse concernant la thématique « Expression et construction de soi » et plus particulièrement l'axe « Mise en scène de soi ».

Document C

Cindy Sherman decided to make her Instagram account public in 2017. This article deals with how the art world responded to that event.

"Cindy prefers not to comment on her Instagram posts."

This was the reply from Cindy Sherman's New York gallery, Metro Pictures, when I asked for a statement. A private Instagram account run by Sherman featuring a new series of selfies was recently made public, creating an art world sensation overnight. Sherman has a long history of dramatically staged self-portraiture, and in a sense pioneered the idea of the "selfie" decades before social media began.

Art world luminaries[1] are fawning over[2] the images, sharing their thoughts in the comments underneath each post. But a mystery still lingers. Part of the confusion is that the work seems to be made specifically for Instagram, and not as a physical work for a future show in a gallery. With no clarification from Sherman herself, it makes for a fascinating quandary[3].

Sherman's Instagram posts are a series of wildly distorted selfies, flower arrangements and disturbing hospital self-portraits, with oxygen tubes up her nostrils. There is a video shot from the perspective of someone lying in a hospital bed. The viewer is made to wonder how much of this is real, whether Sherman was actually hospitalized, or if it's mere fabrication. The images are also affected by an array of decorative filters available on Instagram that animate or change the facial features of users. The line between real life and posed events that Instagram affords heightens the confusion as to what is actually happening.

That area between real life and the theatre of the selfie is what Sherman is already so adept at presenting, but in the context of an era where Donald Trump has repeatedly criticized women for their physical appearance, her images of distorted female faces take on a much more defiant tone.

Sherman's Instagram posts accomplish something not seen in recent years – they hold up a dark mirror to our era of self-obsession. Artist Richard Prince accomplished this with his recent Instagram-themed work, but in a different way. Prince also printed the images for physical exhibitions at Gagosian

Gallery – something Sherman may or may not end up doing. The subsequent legalities associated with Prince's series took his social media interaction in a much different and more controversial direction than Sherman's.

What does our digital landscape mean for the changing nature of exhibiting one's work? Is it better or worse than showing in a real gallery space? "The difference between exhibiting online over exhibiting in a real space is 'depth' in every possible sense," said New York writer and curator Jeffrey Grunthaner. "You can't really take a point of view on an image; there's no genuine scale[4] to it. It's simply there, floating in digitality. There's a certain potential for dictating exactly how viewers look at an artwork that is quite appealing. As I see it, the difficulty in accepting the ascendancy of exhibiting online relates to the proscribed corporate identity most online venues have."

(...)

In many cases, Instagram is not art but a digital dumping ground – a playground for society's worst narcissists. For an artist like Sherman to be using it as an exhibition space raises the bar for users seeking attention or claiming to be artists.

Noah Becker, "How Cindy Sherman's Instagram selfies are changing the face of photography", *The Guardian*, August 2017.

1. luminaries: *personnes éminentes* **2.** to fawn over: *faire l'éloge de manière servile*
3. a quandary: *un dilemme* **4.** scale: *l'échelle*

LE SUJET

Write a short commentary on the three documents (about 500 words): taking into account the specificities of each document, analyse how the three documents use various forms of self-representation as a means of artistic expression to question individual and cultural identities.

LA FEUILLE DE ROUTE

→ *Méthode détaillée de la synthèse dans le chapitre 4, p. 104.*

Étape 1 Analyser les termes du sujet

- *Self representation*: le fait d'utiliser sa propre image, ou de parler de soi dans une œuvre d'art n'est pas anodin. Interrogez-vous sur la spécificité de ce choix dans les œuvres du corpus.
- *Artistic expression*: plusieurs formes d'art apparaissent dans le corpus. Analysez la portée de l'utilisation de l'art comme moyen d'expression dans les trois documents.
- *Individual and cultural identities*: L'identité renvoie à la notion de « soi ». La juxtaposition des termes « individuel » et « collectif » interroge ce concept en lui donnant un sens plus large qu'il faudra analyser.

Étape 2 Lire et analyser le corpus à la lumière de la problématique

- **Problématique**: How is self-portraiture a reflection on both culture and individuality?
- Définir **le point de vue** de chaque document et repérer le lien de chacun avec *self-portraiture*.
- Surligner dans chaque document les **éléments pertinents** par rapport à *individual identity* et *cultural identity*

Étape 3 Analyser et comparer l'apport de chaque document

	Kind of self-portrait	Representation of the self	Cultural elements
Doc A: poem			
Doc B: photograph			
Doc C: article		What is said about Sherman's self-portraits in the article is that they are distorted. Instead of presenting a glamourized version of herself, she uses Instagram filters to appear as ugly.	The article stresses how Sherman uses social media to offer a grim reflection upon the kind of image of women it promotes.

Étape 4 Construire le plan de la synthèse

À partir du tableau, on peut dégager trois axes pour répondre à la problématique:

I. Provocative self-portraits
II. Constructing and deconstructing the self
III. Re-inventing individual and cultural identities through art

Étape 5 Rédiger la synthèse

→ CORRIGÉS p. 61

8 Traduction en français

→ *Méthode détaillée de la traduction dans le chapitre 6, p. 139.*

Traduisez l'extrait de l'article du *Guardian* (texte C), de « Cindy prefers not to comment » (ligne 1) à « future show in a gallery. » (ligne 11).

CONSEIL
Part of the confusion (l. 9-10) : il va être nécessaire d'*étoffer* pour rendre le sens explicite. Repérez pour cela à quoi le mot *confusion* renvoie dans le texte.

CORRIGÉS

SE TESTER QUIZ

1 The expression of emotions

1. a. Abstract expressionism • b. Transcendentalism • c. Romanticism

2. a. Vrai. Some artists, such as Lord Alfred Tennyson, have used their own emotions to create art.
b. Faux. Second generation Romantics also dealt with politics.
c. Vrai. Catharsis first referred to the audience's emotional response to tragedy.
d. Vrai. Many political speeches appeal to the audience's feelings in order to be effective.

2 Staging the self

1. a. a self-portrait • b. the self • c. a slave narrative • d. to witness

2. c. Grayson Perry uses his female alter ego, Claire, throughout his work.

3 Initiation and learning

1. a. Faux. Only young men from the gentry went on the Grand Tour.
b. Vrai. During the Blitz, children had to survive without their parents' protection.
c. Vrai. *Crossing the River*, by Caryl Phillips, focuses on characters who face prejudice and eventually overcome it.

2. Many artists have tried to tackle the coming of age process, but the one genre that most famously did it was the education novel, or bildungsroman. Those novels often focus on a protagonist's mental, psychological and moral development and help the reader understand human nature.

S'ENTRAÎNER

4 Réviser le cours en 8 questions flash

1. Romantics emphasized nature, and individuality in their work. Later Romantics showed interest in politics.

2. Unlike first generation rappers whose songs mostly dealt with partying, Run DMC was one of the first rap bands to make conscious hip hop.

3. While David Hockney's self-portraits offer an intellectual reflection upon the passage of time, Sherman's work aims at deconstructing the notion of the self.

4. Dandyism is the movement represented in *The Picture of Dorian Gray*.

5. Churchill has been accused of distorting reality to serve his own personal and political motives.

6. Franklin's autobiography contributed to the making of the self-made man myth. It has been both praised and decried for that very reason.

7. In *I love Dick*, Chris Kraus raised the issue of the recognition of female artists' work in the 20th century.

8. Symbols, and narratorial comments are often used in education novels to guide the reader through the moral message of the work.

5 Analyser un poème

1.

Provocative	"Turbulent, fleshy, sensual, eating, drinking and breeding," (l. 15)
Empathetic	"Whoever degrades another degrades me," (l. 18) "Voices of the interminable generations of prisoners and slaves," (l. 23)
All-encompassing	"Walt Whitman, a kosmos, of Manhattan the son" (l. 14)

2. Réponses a et b.
As it appears in the very first stanza of the poem, Whitman directly addresses the reader, using the pronoun "you", which is contrasted with the first person pronoun "I" that introduces the poem.
Whitman also addresses the entire nation, America, by mentioning "democracy" (l. 20): here, the poet expresses his will that every American should be heard.
Although many references to the universe and transcendentalist thought are present in the poem, Whitman does not address it to the "cosmos".

3. The literary devices and rhythm used in the poem endow it with the qualities of a song. In "Song of Myself", Whitman uses free verse. Repetitions (or anaphoras) are consistently used in section 24. "Voices" is repeated at the beginning of lines 23 to 32, and the word "and" is repeated in the following two lines.
The subject matter of the poem is the self, which appears throughout the poem as first-person pronouns are iterated over twenty times. However, this needs to be understood within the framework of transcendentalism – Whitman really focuses on the bond that exists between all individuals.

> **INFO**
> **Free verse**: as opposed to more traditional forms of poetry, free verse does not use rhyme schemes or consistent meter patterns.

6 Analyser une image

1. The title of the exhibition uses the imperative and emphasizes the first person pronoun "me". Indeed, the artist's posture and the bright colours used in the picture compel the viewer to look at it.

2. a. Jewelry, makeup and nail polish are usually associated with femininity.
b. In contrast, the policeman's hat is traditionally associated with masculinity.
c. By wearing them all at the same time, Bowery plays with gender.

3. What is most striking in this picture is the use of contrast. The artist's face is painted blue, and vivid colours (red, gold, green, black and yellow) stand in stark contrast with it. The artist's still facial expression contrasts with all the other elements in the picture.

Bowery's use of drag conveys a sense of festivity highlighted by the references to the Indian festival of colours, which celebrates love, and the arrival of spring.

INFO
Drag refers to the wearing of clothing of the opposite gender as a form of self-expression in the LGBTQ+ community.

OBJECTIF BAC

7 Synthèse de documents • *Expression et construction de soi*

Les titres en couleur et les puces permettent de mettre en évidence la structure du corrigé mais ils ne figureraient pas sur une copie de bac.

Introduction

Self-expression can be said to be one of the main purposes of art. The three documents under examination deal with self-portraiture as a seemingly direct way of expressing oneself. They show how the bold move of using oneself as the subject-matter of one's art may lead to a deeper understanding of the notion of identity.

I. Provocative self-portraits

- All three documents present us with "**dramatically staged self-portraits**" (C, l. 5-6): Whitman's poem can be described as a literary self-portrait, Bowery's photograph is an image of the artist in drag, and the Guardian's article discusses Cindy Sherman's use of the selfie on Instagram.
- These sources take us beyond the representation of an artist in a work of art, and **call the very notion of the self into question**: Bowery breaks free from traditional representations of masculinity; Whitman endeavours to re-define the notion of the self; Cindy Sherman's work, as it is discussed in the article, deals with a contemporary representation of the self that is the selfie.
- The **provocative nature** of all the self-portraits under study is rather striking. Whitman's and Bowery's self-portraits present their viewer or reader with a shocking representation of themselves, emphasizing sexuality. Sherman's "distorted selfies" (C, l. 13), as they are discussed in the article, build on a contemporary trend in order to criticize the 'staging' of oneself on social media in the late 2010s.

II. Constructing and deconstructing the self

- From the first line of "Song of Myself", Walt Whitman introduces the first-person pronoun in a celebratory tone: "I celebrate myself, and sing myself" (A, l. 1). This assertion of the self mirrors the title of the exhibition: Bowery's photograph was shown in "Look at me" (B). Both documents use self-representation to introduce a **well-constructed image of the self** to the viewer.
- Sherman's Instagram account, on the other hand, **deconstructs the idea of the self** as Instagram might promote it- she emphasises the fake nature of how people present themselves on Instagram, leading "The viewer (...) to wonder how much of this is real" (C, l. 16) through her use of Instagram filters.

III. Re-inventing individual and cultural identities through art

- **Re-invention of the self** is at the core of this set of documents. Bowery achieves a new identity by borrowing elements from Indian culture and by being in drag. Sherman endlessly distorts her own image on Instagram. In "Song of Myself", Whitman seems to present himself in an arrogant manner but then shifts to speak for others, namely the poor and the weak: "through me many long, dumb voices" (A, l. 22).

> **CONSEIL**
> Les idées de votre synthèse doivent être présentées de manière **progressive**: des plus simples aux plus complexes. Aussi, il vous sera nécessaire de maîtriser plusieurs concepts opérants pour rédiger votre troisième partie.

- All three self-portraits discussed here offer a **comment on the culture in which they were produced**. Bowery's colourful picture is emblematic of the London club scene of the early 1980s. Likewise, Sherman's work needs to be understood within "the context of an era where Donald Trump has repeatedly criticized women for their physical appearance" (C, l. 24): she uses social media to criticize the widespread trend of women feeling they have to appear as perfect. Whitman builds on transcendentalist thought to equate (*assimiler*) collective and individual selves: "For every atom belonging to me as good belongs to you" (A, l. 3).
- While Whitman reinvents American poetry by popularizing free verse, Bowery does so with performance, by becoming a walking work of art. The journalist's point of view in the article seems to be that the true purpose of Sherman is to criticize the shallow use of photography that is widespread on social media, "The difference between exhibiting online over exhibiting in a real space is 'depth'" (C, l. 34-35). Ultimately, it can be said that these documents question their own artform.

Conclusion

Self-portraiture is multidimensional: the three documents underline the complexity of self-representation. "Staging" oneself is a **deceptive means of artistic expression**. Rather than merely portraying the artist, these works actually contribute to creating or recreating culture and art.

8 Traduction en français

« Cindy préfère ne pas faire de commentaire sur ses publications Instagram. »
Voici la réponse que m'a donnée Metro Pictures, la galerie de Cindy Sherman à New York, lorsque j'ai demandé un communiqué. Un compte Instagram privé tenu par Sherman comprenant une série de selfies a récemment été rendu public, et, du jour au lendemain, a fait sensation dans le monde de l'art. Il y a longtemps que Sherman produit des autoportraits mis en scène de manière théâtrale, et, dans une certaine mesure, elle a été l'une des pionnières du concept de selfie plusieurs décennies avant l'avènement des réseaux sociaux.
Les grands noms de l'art s'extasient devant les images, et partagent leurs avis en commentaires des publications. Cependant, un mystère demeure. La confusion produite par l'événement provient en partie du / Une incertitude demeure concernant le fait que ce travail semble avoir été fait spécifiquement pour Instagram, et non en vue d'un travail concret pour une exposition future dans une galerie.

3 Travels, territories, frontiers

Travelling and setting up new frontiers are concepts deeply related to English-speaking countries which all have gained a lot from exploring the world.

13 Great Britain, a nation of explorers

En bref *Over the centuries, Great Britain has proved to be a nation of explorers. This yearning for travels can be explained by many reasons, either political, commercial, or scientific. Discovering the world early appeared as essential for this island nation.*

I Exploring in the name of the ruler

1 Exploring to expand territory and power

- Britain has a long tradition of explorers and navigators. Elizabeth I (1558-1603), first British monarch supporting maritime explorations, commissioned many sailors including Sir Walter Raleigh or Sir Francis Drake, to find new trade routes and lands so as to establish trading outposts and colonies.
- 18th century Britain knew a growing interest in travel narratives responding to the public's appetite for more accurate descriptions of lands and peoples of distant regions. *Captain James Cook's diaries* were published in 1784. After his expeditions in the South Seas, he brought back maps, log books (*journaux de bord*), and paintings to the homes and imaginations of British people.

2 Developing trade and imposing British culture

- David Livingstone was a Scottish missionary and one of the greatest explorers of Africa. He opened up the interior of the continent allowing European nations to explore it. His best-selling *Missionary Travels and Researches in South Africa* (1857) was widely read and translated. Convinced that the introduction of Christianity, commerce and civilisation would free African peoples from slavery, he spent his life exploring that continent.
- And yet, the nation's missions in the colonies were not praised by all. In 1899 Joseph Conrad, both sailor and writer, published his short story *The Heart of Darkness*. It can be read as a political critique of Western **imperialism** which was "just robbery with violence" for him. It was not an exchange of resources, but an unfair usurpation of the wealth of the weaker party by the stronger.

INFO
Imperialism is a system in which a country rules over others, sometimes using force to get power over them.

II Exploring in the name of science

1 Broadening scientific knowledge

- The 19th century saw the birth of science as a profession; the term scientist was coined (*inventé*) in 1833. Among the most influential ideas of that period were those of Charles Darwin.

■ He was an English naturalist who decided to embark on a five-year voyage around the world on the HMS Beagle to study exotic wildlife. As a result of his observations, he proposed the **theory of evolution by natural selection** in the book *On the Origin of Species*, published in 1859.

> **INFO**
> Darwin's **theory of natural selection** states that all species evolve through the survival of the fittest.

■ Challenging the beliefs of that time, his ideas first created controversy in Victorian society. But his work was soon considered as one of the most important science books ever published.

2 | Pushing one's limit

■ At the turn of the 20th century, the Antarctic was still an uncharted (*non cartographié*) area. Sir Ernest Henry Shackleton was one of the numerous British adventurers who allowed greater access to the continent and its occupation by scientific stations. He published his expedition account, *The Heart of the Antarctic* in 1909 and toured the country to popularise his polar journeys.

■ In 1914, Shackleton led the Trans-Antarctic Expedition and managed to rescue all his crew after his ship was crushed by ice. He rapidly became a role model for leadership as one who, in extreme conditions, kept his team together and pushed the limits of physical endurance.

zoOm

Grand Tourists at the Monument of Philopappos

Louis François Cassas, *Grand Tourists at the Monument of Philopappos*, 1821.

Following the 18th century tradition of the Grand Tour, this painting shows travellers desiring to broaden their knowledge and experience by visiting Europe.

→ Read more about the tradition of the *Grand Tour*: bit.ly/PbacAngTle_13a

14 The USA, on the move forever

En bref *American history is largely based on conquests and redefining the Frontier. The American identity has been shaped by women and men on the go, ready to fulfil their dreams and craving for adventure and freedom.*

I Forging a nation

1 A new identity

- In 1804, the Louisiana Territory purchase from France led President Thomas Jefferson to commission the Lewis and Clark expedition. After a two-year journey, the two explorers managed to reach the Pacific Coast providing new geographical, ecological and social information about previously uncharted areas of North America. They gave a detailed account of their journey and discoveries in their *Journals of the Lewis and Clark Expedition*.

- This expedition paved the way to the westward expansion. The Manifest Destiny expressed the belief that the Americans were destined by God to spread civilisation over the continent and became its driving force. By the mid-19th century a shift of population (*déplacement de population*) took place, millions of settlers decided to try their luck and headed West.

2 Life on the Frontier

- Expecting easy fortune and an adventurous life in the West, many families took advantage of **the Homestead Act** and became land owners known as homesteaders. But as the territory was often unknown and peopled by Natives defending their land, frontiersmen had to face many dangers.

> **INFO**
> **The Homestead Act** (1862) enabled settlers to get land in the West for free, provided they built a home and improved the property for five years.

- James Fenimore Cooper depicted life on the Frontier in his novels, but his greatest gift was in conveying the image of prototypical American landscapes of forests, lakes, and prairies, and of the free men who lived there. He thus introduced Americans to their own Frontier. His most important work, *The Last of the Mohicans* (1826) portrays white and Native American interactions.

II Hitting the road: a thirst for freedom

1 Escaping conventions

- Jack Kerouac's novel *On the Road* (1957) is based on his travels across the US and is considered a defining work of the **Beat generation**.

INFO

The Beat generation: young people in the 1950s who rejected literary formalism, and materialism. They valued all types of explorations.

- It inspired generations of readers, writers and artists to take the road for existential or even spiritual journeys of their own. "The road is life," is one oft-quoted phrase from *On the Road*. America is a country of immigrants whose history is irrevocably linked to that of the road.
- But in the 1950s it was the quest for non-conformity that appealed to people, and the need to rebel. The idea of rebelling then became tied to that of travelling – of gaining freedom and independence through running away and exploring the world, away from society's expectations.

2 Looking for their American dream

- The cult "road movie" *Easy Rider* (Dennis Hopper, 1969) is also an ode to freedom. Two freewheeling motorcyclists are riding on decorated Harley-Davidson choppers across a conformist and corrupt America. The movie highlights the sociological changes the American society underwent at the time.
- Rather than travelling westward on horses as the frontiersmen did, the two modern-day cowboys travel eastward from Los Angeles – the end of the traditional Frontier – to New Orleans, on an epic journey into the unknown looking for their "American dream".

zoOm

Expansion at the expense of the Natives

Max D. Standley, *The Trail of Tears*, 1995.

The Removal Act (1830) led to forced displacements imposed on Natives: they had to leave their home territory and live on reservations. They were thus forced to give up their nomadic way of life.

→ Read more about the Trail of Tears: bit.ly/PbacAngTle_14a

15 Cultural bondage and identity

En bref *One's identity is closely linked to the place one comes from or lives. Sharing a common heritage and culture enhances one's sense of belonging to a specific place and community. It can lead to a deep sense of pride in one's roots, culture, country, region, town or place.*

I A strong sense of belonging

1 Patriotism

- Words like fatherland, motherland or homeland show the strong emotional link between people and the country they are from. People are proud of their national identity. In *Ivanhoe* (1819), Walter Scott creates the national myth of the fusion of Normans and Saxons into a united English people. By bringing opposed interests together, a single identity is forged.

- As Rupert Brooke's poem *The Soldier* (1915) stresses, England is a treasure to hold dear, worth fighting for and dying for. The soldier's death even adds to its glory.

2 Celebrating one's culture and heritage

- People celebrate their culture and heritage through literature, arts, sport, and even food. It enables them to claim their identity and to show how proud of their roots they are. Such is the case with the Celtic Revival in the 19th and 20th centuries, whose main concerns were Ireland's historic past, its myths, legends and folklore. Poet and playwright William Butler Yeats was a driving force of that literary movement.

- People rally around their cultural heritage. The Highland Games, yearly traditional events, embody the link that bonds Scottish people together. So do such traditions as **Robert Burns Night** on the 25th of January. That strong sense of belonging is also expressed whenever *Flower of Scotland* by the Corries (1967) is sung at rugby matches.

INFO
During **Robert Burns Night**, Scottish people gather together for a special supper, which includes reading Robert Burn's poem *Address to a Haggis* and traditional dance.

II Transmission of traditional heritage

1 Landmarks

- To maintain that sense of belonging, it is necessary to transmit traditional heritage. Such is the role of the American National Park Service in the USA or of the National Trust in Great Britain which is a charity devoted to maintaining and developing historical, cultural and natural heritage.

■ Artists contribute to that transmission too: John Constable painted idyllic country landscapes as in *The Hay Wain* (1821), thus transmitting his love for rural life. Thomas Hardy also chanted country life and nature in his poems, thus portraying the place he belongs. Commemorating the past partakes of the same process: Poppy Day marks the end of World War I and pays tribute to the many soldiers who died in Flanders as first portrayed in John McCrae's poem *In Flanders Fields* (1915).

2 Sharing one's culture

■ The sense of belonging is affected by migration. It is important to preserve the link with one's roots. Yet, it is equally important to share one's culture to contribute to building a new national identity. It is at stake in Benjamin Zephaniah's poem *The British* (2000). Similarly, the Notting Hill Carnival in London celebrates West Indian culture and highlights the contribution of the Afro-Caribbean community to British culture. It is considered as an icon of Britain.

■ Black History Month, every February in the USA since 1976, and the National Museum of African American History in Washington since 2016, have enabled Afro-Americans to claim their past heritage, to show how they contributed to building the nation and to stress their role in American history.

zoOm

Ray Charles and *Georgia on My Mind*

Ray Charles was made to feel unwelcomed in segregated Georgia after he refused to play for an all white audience in 1961 in Atlanta. He sang *Georgia on My Mind*, a 1930 popular folklore song, for the first time in 1960. It became Georgia's hymn in 1976.

→ Listen to the song: bit.ly/PbacAngTle_15a

16 Cultural heritage, a bone of contention

En bref *As it is linked to a specific territory, cultural heritage can also trigger division and conflict. A frontier marks the boundary between places and it may prove vital to defend and protect both territory and cultural heritage against other threatening countries and cultures.*

I A matter of survival

1 Overcoming colonialism

- Indigenous people lost their territory because of colonialism: the Native Peoples of America were forced to live on reservations and to give up their nomadic way of life. So as to survive as distinct peoples, they had to maintain their language and oral traditions, even secretly.

- The Maori people also had to cling to their roots to preserve their cultural identity. Although the meaning of tattoos may be confusing, there is a growing interest in that tradition which is now promoted. In *The Bone People* (1984), Keri Hulme denounces the clash between Maori and European cultures. Yet, she promotes cultural unity in order to heal New Zealand from its cultural illness.

2 Reclaiming one's territory and culture

- The Aborigines in Australia are still fighting to defend their territory against the invasion of tourists who trample (*piétinent*) over their culture when hiking on their sacred lands. It is vital for them to preserve that fragile cultural heritage.

- That culture almost disappeared because of **forced assimilation**: Aboriginal children, referred to as the Stolen Generation, were deprived of their parents, culture and language. Films such as *Walkabout* (1971) or *Australia* (2008) claim the necessity to maintain Aboriginal traditions.

> **INFO**
> **Forced assimilation** refers to indigenous peoples being forced to adopt the language, norms, customs, traditions and values of the English settlers.

II The great divide

1 An invisible border

- The frontier between territories may appear as an impenetrable barrier between cultures. It marks the clear-cut difference between contrasting ways of life. The difference between rural and urban landscapes epitomizes the cultural gap between rural and urban ways of life. In "Mowing" (1913) and "The Sound of Trees" (1916) American poet Robert Frost portrays rural life and exposes urban life as both complicated and less meaningful.

■ The boundary between the North and the South in a particular country may not be that obvious for it is not clearly visible. Yet, there is a gap as Elizabeth Gaskell's novel *North and South* (1855) describes it. She confronts modern industrial thriving (*prospère*) Northern England and out-dated Southern England.

2 | A yawning chasm

■ Landscapes may be scarred by conflicts over territories and cultures that cannot be solved. Such has been the case of Northern Ireland ever since the partition of Ireland in 1921 although a political status quo has put an end to armed conflict. Belfast's murals are a vivid testimony of the gap between its two communities. In *Everything in this Country Must* (2000) Colum McCann focuses on the everlasting effects on individuals on both sides.

■ It seems that there is a yawning chasm (*gouffre béant*) between irreconcilable parties and that it is forever visible on maps. The ingrained racism of the Southern states of the USA is at the heart of *Everything That Rises Must Converge* by Flannery O'Connor (1965) as the main characters seem unable to adjust to the new integrated South. Even American towns geographically map that enduring social segregation.

zoOm

Climbing ban on Uluṟu

Uluṟu is not just a tourist destination but a symbol of the Aboriginal struggle for land rights. Once appropriated by the Australian government for tourism and renamed "Ayers Rock", it is now a model for collaborative indigenous-governmental land management as the climbing ban issued in 2010 shows it.

→ Read more about Aboriginal people: bit.ly/PbacAngTle_16a

17 Multifaceted migration and exile

En bref *There have always been the same types and forms of migration triggered by the same circumstances and reasons. Yet, whether people choose to migrate or not, they do so somehow reluctantly. Some even experience exile without leaving and being expatriated.*

I Having to leave

1 For economic reasons

■ Dire poverty (*l'extrême pauvreté*) makes people leave their home in search of a better place. The Great Potato Famine (1845-1852) started a long process of Irish migration to the USA. For example, Frank McCourt's memoir, *Angela's Ashes* (1996), stresses his family left because of destitution. The same reasons lead people from South America to endure a long hazardous journey to the USA.

■ Similarly, the Oakies in John Steinbeck's novel *The Grapes of Wrath* (1939) flee their home to try their luck in California because of drought, economic hardship and bank foreclosures (*saisies*).

> **INFO**
> **The Oakies** were destitute people forced to abandon their farms and migrate to California, when Oklahoma was hit by severe dust storms in the 1930s.

2 For social and political reasons

■ Colonialism and the rise and fall of the British Empire are closely linked to migration and exile. In an attempt to deal with overcrowded prisons, Britain sent convicts (*prisonniers*) away to settle in Australia. Such is the main theme of *Botany Bay* by Charles Nordhoff and James Norman Hall (1941). Besides, decolonisation triggered such drastic changes and violence in former British colonies that it entailed migration back to Great Britain.

■ People can be driven out of their homes by conflicts and wars. The official poster "Women Wanted for Evacuation Service" shows British children who were evacuated during the Blitz. Many people, such as the Jews who ran away to escape pogroms in Eastern Europe and the Holocaust, also flee religious and / or political persecution. It's the case of Beverley Naidoo's young characters who flee Nigeria and take refuge in Britain in *The Other Side of Truth* (2000).

II Being exiled at home

1 No sense of belonging

■ People who leave their home feel as exiles. Consequently, many emigrants, and even their children who were born and bred in their adopted country, dream of returning to their country of origin.

■ Yet, it often proves a baffling (*déroutante*) experience for those who attempt it: they realise they are foreigners in their ancestors' land. Colm Tóibín's main character in *Brooklyn* (2009) does not feel at home either in the US where she chose to settle or Ireland when she comes back.

INFO
Exiles live away from home. They face obstacles (language, integration) and a sense of alienation (nostalgia, uprootedness).

■ Being in between two worlds and cultures is also experienced by Native Americans as Sherman Alexie points out in *Indian Killer* (1996). They do not belong and are neither Natives nor Americans.

2 Exile from within

■ That feeling of estrangement is even worse for people who have not even left their own country. They may have been displaced to another part of it like Native Americans on the Trail of Tears → FICHE 14 and they may have undergone forced assimilation like the Stolen Generation in Australia → FICHE 16. That form of exile is illustrated in *Rabbit Proof Fence* (2002) by Phillip Noyce adapted from Doris Pilkington's novel.

■ Nadine Gordimer and André Brink chose to remain in South Africa while taking sides with Black people under Apartheid. They were thus forced to exile within their own country: they were subjected to severe censorship. *Burger's Daughter* and *A Dry White Season* (1979) were banned in South Africa.

zoOm

"Home Children"

In a seventy-year period (1869-1939), more than 100,000 British orphans were sent to Canada from England, Scotland, Ireland, and Wales. Those young exiles often became unpaid farmhands and servants, and many were ill-treated. British Prime Minister Gordon Brown apologized for that inhumane past policy in 2010.

→ Read more on child migration history: bit.ly/PbacAngTle_17a

18 Migrating for better or for worse

En bref *Migrating entails adjusting to a new place and culture, which may prove difficult especially when one has to fight to settle or to face discrimination and xenophobia. Immigrants may feel lost and uprooted (*déracinés*). Yet, it can be successful when they fulfil their dreams.*

I A tough experience

1 Rejected and uprooted

- Adapting to a new place and culture is hard when facing rejection and xenophobia. It is even harder when it means fighting over a territory as Martin Scorcese's film *Gangs of New York* (2002) shows with the deadly fight between Catholic Irish immigrants and earlier Protestant settlers in Manhattan.
- Hanif Kureishi's *The Buddha of Suburbia* (1990) stresses the confusion and bewilderment (*incompréhension*) migrants experience when settling in another country. Hence, some feel safer by clinging to their traditions. It is the choice of the main character's parents who fear British culture and remain within their own communities in Gurinder Chadha's film *Bend it like Beckham* (2002). People feel all the more uprooted as it is hard for them to find their place and build their identity anew. In *Americanah* (2013) by Chimamanda Ngozi Adichie, Ifemelu goes back to Nigeria after struggling to adapt to the US for thirteen years.

2 Traumatic wandering

- Diasporic people live in a paradoxical condition: cut off and haunted by their past at the same time. Many black artists have explored the constant trauma of the **Middle Passage**.

> **INFO**
> **The Middle Passage** refers to the Transatlantic forced migration of African people to America on slave ships.

- Dionne Brand, an Afro-Caribbean Canadian writer focuses on displaced rootless individuals and the trauma of exile. In *A Map of the Door of No Return* (2001), she portrays black diasporic people trapped between an unforgettable traumatic past and an unfathomable (*insondable*) future.

II A positive experience

1 Positive transmutation

- As hybrid individuals caught between two races and cultures, second-generation immigrants often feel trapped too. In *How the Garcia Girls Lost their Accents* by Julia Alvarez (1991), Yolanda embarks on a journey of self-exploration. It allows her to embrace her fractured self.

■ **Postcolonial novelist** Salman Rushdie rejects the British colonial portrayal of India and builds a new world. He fuses the idea of magic and reality through a new technique called magic realism. Instead of seeking to recover lost traditional motherland, his characters accept hybridity as a way to find a new balanced identity.

> **INFO**
> **Postcolonial writers** are from formerly colonised countries. They often address the problems and consequences of the decolonisation of a country.

■ Finding one's balance through the mixing of Western and indigenous cultures is Chris Ofili's concern too. He usually mixes Western and Nigerian iconography and references on one canvas *(toile)*, to suggest multiplicity and diversity blend in one space.

2 | A dream come true

■ Settling in another country offers new opportunities: people can begin afresh and benefit from better living conditions as is sung by the Corrs in *Ellis Island* (2015). It enables them to experience new freedoms as is developed by Monica Ali in *Brick Lane* (2003).

■ Even if it started in order to flee dire poverty and segregation in the South, *The Great Migration* (1916-1970) painted by Jacob Lawrence in *The Migration Series* (1941) eventually enabled Black Americans to build a new place for themselves in public life, to get more power and to create an influential urban culture.

zoOm

UK Diaspora

Kimathi Donkor discusses his artwork "UK Diaspora" (2007) which questions the depiction of great national figures such as John Hawkins, British slave trader, Queen Elizabeth I, or George Washington who all had connections to the Transatlantic slave trade. He hopes to make people wonder if these dignified icons really deserve to be represented in this high esteem.

→ Watch the video: bit.ly/PbacAngTle_18a

Kimathi Donkor, illustration exposée à la Foire 1-54 de Londres en octobre 2015.

MÉMO VISUEL

- **Territory:** a place one belongs to, part of one's identity and culture, but also an object of pride that needs to be shared to strengthen one's sense of belonging.
- **Cultural heritage:** is linked to a particular territory which can be cherished or preserved, which one can defend or die for.
- **Loss of landmarks:** leaving one's country creates a feeling of confusion, a trauma or an in-between state.

Key ideas

Travels, territorie

Exploration and adventure

Great Britain, a nation of explorers

In the late 1500s, Elizabeth I supported maritime explorations which led to the adventure of colonising America and the development of new worldwide trade routes.

The USA, a country on the move forever

After the Lewis and Clark expedition, the entire country looked West. Millions of people hit the road and settled wherever free land was to be found.

Cultural anchoring and heritage

Cultural bondage and identity
The Notting Hill Carnival in London celebrates West Indian culture and illustrates the idea of plurality at the core of British identity.

Cultural heritage, a bone of contention
Native peoples like the Aborigines in Australia are still struggling to protect their land from depredation and striving to maintain their culture alive.

rontiers

Migration and exile

Multifaceted migration and exile
Millions of Irish people were driven out of their native land forever because of the Potato Famine in the 19th century or the Troubles in the 20th century.

Migrating for better or for worse
Diasporic people feel uprooted and rejected as they are neither from here nor from there but manage to fit in by embracing their very hybridity.

SE TESTER QUIZ

Vérifiez que vous avez bien compris les points clés des **fiches 13 à 18**.

1 Exploration and adventure

→ FICHES 13 ET 14

1. Retrouvez un synonyme pour chacun des mots ou groupe de mots suivants.

a. in the West (adj) : ....
b. an explorer (n) : ....
c. a trip (n) : ....
d. a land owner (n) : ....

2. Associez chaque œuvre à son genre.

a. *Missionary Travels and Researches in South Africa* by D. Livingstone •	• an expedition account
b. *The Last of the Mohicans* by J.F. Cooper •	• a novel
c. *Heart of the Antarctic* by E.H. Shackleton •	• a travel narrative

2 Cultural anchoring and heritage

→ FICHES 15 ET 16

Vrai ou faux ? Cochez la case qui convient.	**V**	**F**
a. Poppy Day is celebrated to pay tribute to the soldiers who died during WWI.	☐	☐
b. The Celtic Revival's main concerns were Ireland's historic past.	☐	☐
c. The conflict over territories and culture in Ireland is now over.	☐	☐
d. Only Aborigines from Australia had to endure forced assimilation.	☐	☐

3 Migration and exile

→ FICHES 17 ET 18

1. Trouvez les mots qui correspondent aux définitions suivantes.

a. Feeling of people displaced from native or habitual surroundings = U_ _ _ _ _ _ _ _ _ _ _ _
b. To migrate to and organise an area = to S_ _ _ _ _
c. A person who is separated from his or her native land = E_ _ _ _

2. Complétez le texte ci-dessous avec les mots qui conviennent.

No matter the reasons why people have to leave home and .... in another place, it is always reluctantly. They feel so .... that they find it hard to adjust to an .... territory and culture. This exile is a real .... that affects first generation migrants and generations after that. Some manage to get over it and eventually fit in while others prove unable to .... and remain .... forever.

S'ENTRAÎNER

4 Réviser le cours en 8 questions flash

1. Who faced controversy after publishing his theory on evolution?
2. What country decided to sell the Louisiana Territory to the USA?
3. How did the Americans justify their westward expansion?
4. What does Walter Scott's national myth consist in?
5. How can African Americans show their various contributions to the building of the American nation?
6. Where can we find visual representations of an unsolved conflict over territory and culture?
7. Who were the Oakies and what were they forced to do?
8. What is the distinctive feature of diasporic people?

5 Analyser une image

→ FICHE 23

Lisez la planche de bande dessinée et répondez aux questions.

Document A

Jin Wang and his family have just moved to a new neighbourhood.

American Born Chinese, Gene Luen Yang (2006) © First Second.

1. Focus on the author's name and the title of the comic book. What do they reveal about the subject and point of view of the story?

2. When related to the title of the comic book, the sentence "with the scent of our old home still lingering on my clothes" suggests that Jin Wang...

- ☐ **a.** ...has just arrived from China and feels uprooted and lost.
- ☐ **b.** ...used to live in a Chinese area and feels uprooted and culturally different.
- ☐ **c.** ...used to live in a Chinese area and is shown as an alien who has to fit in.

3. How can you interpret the teacher's mistakes and the pupils' facial expressions?

6 Comprendre un poème

→ FICHE 20

Lisez le poème et répondez aux questions.

Document B

Pat Mora is a Mexican-American poet who uses her own experience to speak for those like her.

Legal Alien

Bi-lingual, Bi-cultural,
able to slip from "How's life?"
to "*Me'stanvolviendo loca,*"[1]
able to sit in a paneled office
drafting memos in smooth English,
able to order in fluent Spanish
at a Mexican restaurant,
American but hyphenated[2],
viewed by Anglos as perhaps exotic,
perhaps inferior, definitely different,
viewed by Mexicans as alien,
(their eyes say, "You may speak
Spanish but you're not like me")
an American to Mexicans
a Mexican to Americans
a handy token[3]
sliding back and forth
between the fringes of both worlds
by smiling
by masking the discomfort
of being pre-judged
Bi-laterally.

Pat Mora, "Legal Alien", in *Chants* (1985) © ARTE PÚBLICO PRESS 2020.

1. Me'stanvolviendo loca: they're driving me nuts
2. hyphenated: of mixed origin or identity
3. token: sample, item, element

1. Complete this chart to show how being a Mexican-American is presented.

	Quotes / examples	Effect / comment
Asset		
Turning point		
Disadvantage		
ID crisis?		

2. Here are the definitions of “bilateral”. Are all definitions suitable?

☐ **a.** Having or involving two sides; affecting both sides.
☐ **b.** Affecting or undertaken by two parties, mutual.
☐ **c.** Having identical sides or parts on each side of an axis, symmetrical.

What can you deduce from it: what does being Mexican-American imply?

3. How is this idea conveyed through the title, structure and rhythm of the poem?

HELP
- Count the sentences and say what effect it has.
- What is similar in the first and last lines?
- Why is the title an oxymoron?

7 Comprendre un texte d'idées → FICHE 22

Lisez le texte et répondez aux questions.

Document C

Aisha Harris is a culture editor at the New York Times. She explains how a trip to Kenya changed the way she thinks about the terms African-American and black American.

One of the first times I recall being asked the question “Where are you from?” was also one of the first times I realized that being black wasn't a sufficient answer. (...) I knew my ethnicity, but where were my ancestors from? (...)

I *am* at least partially African, genetically speaking. A few years ago, my father took an ancestry DNA test, which revealed that some of his roots can be traced to Nigeria. But I don't consider myself Nigerian-American, or even African-American. Where I'm from is America—who I am is a black American.

I was about 7 or 8 when my dad sat me down to watch *Roots*—all 500 hours of it. (...) Alex Haley's tale of genealogical discovery resonated with my father as a powerful attempt to re-establish the lineal connection between Africans and African-Americans that had been erased by slavery. *Roots* was just one of the African-themed cultural artifacts that my father introduced to my sister and me. (...) He attempted to instill in us not just a sense of pride as black Americans, but as Americans of African descent, and throughout my adolescence, I identified as black and African-American interchangeably. All of this without knowing, at the time, from what country our ancestors had come, due to the loss and erasure of their birth records prior to the turn of the 20th century.

Despite my father's efforts, however, my first in-depth encounters with first- and second-generation Americans who had immediate family from African countries made me question my adherence to the label of African-American. To me, people with such explicit connections to their relatives' home countries accurately embody the term; they truly have access to both cultures. As someone who grew up with a much stronger sense of my black American roots, and an understanding of African culture distilled primarily through an American sensibility, I feel as though the term *African-American* doesn't quite suit my identity. (...)

I (...) am comfortable (...) with defining myself by my upbringing rather than by where my ancestors may have come from. (...)

Having never lived in the land of my ancestors, I will never truly understand what it means to be Kenyan, Nigerian, or, more generally, African. But my recent travels (...) gave me my first immersive understanding of an African country [Kenya], and I did feel a kinship[1] with the people I met: It was fascinating to spend time in a country where the majority of the population was not white, and to interact with such a wide range of social classes and cultures, from the traditional Maasai tribes to the rural farmers and city dwellers. Finally, after years of learning from afar, I got to understand a small slice of African culture for myself.

Aisha Harris, "Where I'm from", Slate.com, July 29th 2014, D.R.

1. kinship: affinity, link

1. The way Aisha Harris considers herself has evolved. Use two different colours to highlight what relates to the two stages she's been through.

Aisha's vision of her identity as a teenager
Aisha's vision of her identity as an adult

2. Use your findings to complete this chart about how the way Aisha Harris defines her identity has evolved.

	Adolescence	**Adulthood**
Identity	... = ...	... ≠ ...
Origins		
Why?		

HELP
How do you understand African-American and black American? Similar or not?

3. Line 38 to the end: What effect did her trip to Kenya have on her?
- ☐ **a.** It made her genuinely understand partially what being African means.
- ☐ **b.** It made her aware of her connection with African people.
- ☐ **c.** It made her consider Africa as home.

OBJECTIF BAC

8 Synthèse de documents • *Voyages, territoires, frontières*

Vous avez 3 heures 30 pour réaliser la synthèse et faire la traduction proposée. C'est à vous de vous organiser pour produire l'ensemble dans le temps imparti.

Les trois documents A (p. 79), B (p. 80) et C (p. 81) que vous venez d'étudier et le document qui va suivre (D) constituent l'ensemble de documents à analyser pour l'épreuve de synthèse concernant la thématique « Voyages, territoires, frontières » et plus particulièrement l'axe « Ancrage et héritage ».

LE SUJET

Write a commentary on the four documents (about 500 words): taking into account their specificities, analyse how the four documents deal with the theme of biculturalism and its consequences for hyphenated Americans.

Document D

Priya is a college student in her late teens. She was born and brought up in Chicago.

"Assimilation is a betrayal of your skin," Priya explained to her father.

"How can it be a betrayal of your skin to work hard and do well?"

"Do well – at what cost? And on whose terms?"

Her father looked around their home (five bedrooms, swimming-pool, three-car garage) and smiled. "It's nice that you have the luxury of your opinions," he said. (...)

"The mistake you made," she told him, "was in moving to America all those years ago."

"You would have preferred to grow up in India?" (...)

"The more I think about it... yes," said Priyamvada. "There is a strength in being brown in a brown country."

"And what is that?"

"Well, look at the way we are treated here."

"Meritocratic promotions, good education, nice homes?" He didn't say it but Priya knew he also meant: his country-club membership, his partnership in a multinational accounting firm, and the fact that both his children studied in universities that had groomed[1] American presidents.

"Not that stuff," she said. "You're always focusing on material comforts, ignoring everything else. Here in America, nice stores treat whites better, and blondes best. In a brown country, everyone looks at each other with respect and feels the bond that comes from having the same color skin. There, there is a sense of pride about their own history, a refusal to cater[2] to Eurocentric notions of the world, a joy that comes from being perfectly centered culturally... Are you *laughing*?"

"No, no," her father said hastily.

"You are. I can't believe this. You are not taking me seriously..."

"Come on, Priya," her father said. "You've got to understand, there is a vast gap between the social theories they preach in the universities and the realities outside. You've got to understand this... (...) If you're so sure of your ideas," he said, "why don't you go visit India and see for yourself?"

Lavanya Sankaran, "Alphabet Soup" in *The Red Carpet*

1. had groomed: had prepared
2. cater to: meet demands, satisfy

▶▶▶ LA FEUILLE DE ROUTE

→ *Méthode détaillée de la synthèse dans le chapitre 4, p. 104.*

Étape 1 Analyser les termes du sujet

- *Biculturalism*: le fait d'être biculturel, d'avoir deux cultures.
- *Hyphenated-Americans*: citoyens américains ayant des origines étrangères.
- *Consequences*: répercussions engendrées par cet état (= *biculturalism*).

Étape 2 Lire et analyser le corpus à la lumière de la problématique

- Problématique: How does biculturalism affect hyphenated-Americans' everyday lives and identities?
- Définir le point de vue de chaque document et repérer le lien de chacun avec *hyphenated American*.
- Surligner dans chaque document les éléments pertinents par rapport à *biculturalism* et *consequences*.

Étape 3 Analyser et comparer l'apport de chaque document

	Who?	Everyday life problem	Identity crisis	Solutions?
Doc A: Graphic novel	• Chinese-American • 2nd generation immigrant • bilingual and bicultural but Chinese upbringing mainly			
Doc B: Poem				

	Who?	Everyday life problem	Identity crisis	Solutions?
Doc C: Editorial (extract)		• "Where are you from?" so black American is not enough	• shifting identity according to time and influences • unclear and incomplete identity	
Doc D: Short story (extract)	• Indian American • 2nd generation immigrant • American upbringing		• feels her identity is incomplete and corrupted by American materialism • looks for her Indian roots • rejects assimilation • considers India as an Eldorado	• need to go to India to reconnect with her roots • is it going to solve her identity crisis and to make her accept her bicultural identity?

Étape 4 Construire le plan de la synthèse

À partir du tableau, on peut dégager trois axes pour répondre à la problématique :

I. Being a hyphenated American and its everyday consequences

II. Identity crisis and sense of belonging?

III. Redefining one's identity: resolution?

Étape 5 Rédiger la synthèse

→ CORRIGÉS p. 89

9 Traduction en français

→ *Méthode détaillée de la traduction dans le chapitre 6, p. 139.*

LE SUJET

Traduisez de « Assimilation is a betrayal of our skin » (ligne 1) à « at the way we are treated here » (ligne 13), de l'extrait de *Alphabet Soup* de Lavanya Sankaran (texte D).

CONSEILS

- Variez les verbes introductifs du discours pour éviter les répétitions.
- Faut-il traduire *looked around* au sens propre ou au sens figuré ?
- Pensez aux divers types de transposition, et à la modulation pour *skin*.

CORRIGÉS

SE TESTER QUIZ

1 Exploration and adventure

1. a. western • b. an adventurer • c. journey • d. homesteader

2. a. *Missionary Travels and Researches in South Africa:* a travel narrative
b. *The Last of the Mohicans:* a novel
c. *Heart of the Antarctic:* an expedition account

2 Cultural anchoring and heritage

Statements a and b are correct.
Statement c is false: the armed conflict is over, but the problem and effects of partition will probably never be solved.
Statement d is false. Aborigines as well as Native peoples of North America had to endure forced assimilation.

3 Migration and exile

1. a. uprootedness • b. to settle • c. exile

2. No matter the reasons why people have to leave home and settle in another place, it is always reluctantly. They feel so uprooted that they find it hard to adjust to an alien territory and culture. This exile is a real trauma that affects first generation migrants and generations after that. Some manage to get over it and eventually fit in while others prove unable to adapt and remain exiles for ever.

S'ENTRAÎNER

4 Réviser le cours en 8 questions flash

1. Charles Darwin faced controversy after publishing his book *On the Origin of Species* (1859).

2. France sold that Territory to the USA in 1804.

3. It was justified with the Manifest Destiny: the idea that the USA had a superior and divine mission to bring democracy and civilisation to the West.

4. With *Ivanhoe*, Walter Scott forged a national myth based on the synthesis of England from Norman and Saxon peoples.

5. The many contributions of black people to American culture are displayed in a special museum in Washington, or shown during the Black History Month.

6. Belfast's murals (Northern Ireland) illustrate the complicated history and culture of this territory, and relate the conflict opposing Nationalists and Republicans.

7. In the 1930s, the Oakies had to give up their farms in Oklahoma because of a severe drought and economic crisis. They migrated to California to start afresh.

8. They both feel cut off and haunted by their ancestors' traumatic experience of the Middle Passage, the forced migration of African people to America.

5 Analyser une image

1. The title implies a Chinese-American's adventure. The author's name clearly suggests that he is himself Chinese-American so the graphic novel is likely to give a genuine vision of biculturalism and its consequences.

2. b and c are the correct answers as he was born in the USA but was brought up according to the Chinese way of life; he has just moved to a new area and a new school and he will have to adjust and fit in.

3. The teacher's mistakes show that she is prejudiced: she considers him as a newly arrived immigrant. For her, he looks Chinese so he is Chinese. The pupils' puzzled faces stress that he probably is the only Chinese-American in the class. They are all staring at him and some even look slightly hostile. The boy with his hand up is even frowning so we can guess his question or comment will not be friendly and will show how biased and prejudiced he is. Jin Wang's introduction to the class is a complete failure as it singles him out as culturally different, as not American instead of helping him fit in this new environment.

6 Comprendre un poème

1.	Quote / example	Effect / interpretation
Asset	• "able to" 3x • "smooth", "fluent": 2 positive adjectives • 2 languages in the same clause	mastering two languages and cultures in various situations and places
Turning point	"American but hyphenated"	shift of tone
Disadvantage	"viewed by" 2x: • 1 positive adjective ("exotic") • then 2 negative adjectives ("inferior", "different") + "alien" + "you're not like me" • intensifiers "perhaps", "definitely" • l. 14-15: binary structure + chiasmus + identical rhythm	• assets turned into disadvantages due to other people's viewpoints • reasonable doubt to certainty: people's opinions cannot evolve • paradox: bilingual and bicultural yet not considered as fully American or fully Mexican
ID crisis?	• "a handy token": metaphor • "sliding back and forth" • "between the fringes of both worlds" • "smiling" then negative words: "masking the discomfort"	• one individual for a whole group who can play different parts cf. abilities quoted before; easy shift from one culture to another • not at the heart of these worlds but outside: an in-between state • 2 contrasting aspects: attitude vs feelings. Overall negative effect

2. All the definitions are suitable so being Mexican American means having a double identity and culture. It can be both an asset and a disadvantage. It definitely means oscillating between two different worlds and personalities, having the feeling of belonging to both worlds and to none altogether so having to face an identity crisis indeed. **However**, the idea of symmetry also suggests a certain balance in an in-between state, however uncomfortable it may be.
3. The **rhythm and structure** of the poem match that very idea. The **hyphens** that have been added in the first and last lines of the poem confirm the idea of an identity crisis which is announced in the oxymoric title. Yet, the poem is a 22-line stanza with **only one sentence** meant to be read in one breath which stresses the idea of unity. The **use of free verse** which conveys a conversational tone shows the perpetual oscillating movement between those two symmetrical aspects of biculturalism is trivial.

7 Comprendre un texte d'idées

1. and 2.

	Adolescence	Adulthood
Identity	Black American = African-American (l. 16)	Black American ≠ African-American (l. 7-8)
Origins	Knew her ethnicity but not where her ancestors were from because of missing records (l. 17-19)	From America (l. 8) Partially African (l. 5) Ancestors from Nigeria (l. 7)
Why?	Her father used ***Roots*** as a means to reestablish the connection between Africans and African-Americans that had been erased by slavery. He tried to instill in her a sense of pride as black American and American of African descent (l. 9-14)	Her encounters with first and second generation African-Americans made her realize she had an understanding of African culture through an American sensibility and did not truly have access to African culture (l. 23-25) "My upbringing rather than by where my ancestors may have come from" (l. 29-30)

3. a and b "I got to understand a small side of African culture for myself" (l. 39-40), "I did feel a kinship with the people I met" (l. 34).

INFO
Roots is a 500-hour TV series based on Alex Haley's novel dramatizing his family saga from his ancestor's enslavement to the liberation of his descendants.

OBJECTIF BAC

8 Synthèse de documents • *Voyages, territoires, frontières*

Les titres en couleur et les puces permettent de mettre en évidence la structure du corrigé mais ils ne figureraient pas sur une copie de bac.

Introduction

The USA is a nation of immigrants whose inhabitants of mixed origins are hyphenated Americans. It is assumed that being bicultural means comfort and proficiency in both cultures. The four documents under study are about hyphenated Americans from different origins coping with biculturalism and its consequences. They show how this status affects their everyday life and leads to questioning their identity, so they try to find solutions to solve this identity crisis.

I. Being a hyphenated American and its everyday consequences.

- Gene Luen Yang's graphic novel and Pat Mora's poem focus on second-generation immigrants. As hyphenated Americans, they are bicultural and bilingual, "able to slip from" one language to the other and thus embrace both cultures. Yet, these assets are turned into disadvantages because of prejudice: for Mrs Greeder, Jin Wang looks Chinese so is Chinese. The poem's persona is "American but hyphenated" and considered "inferior, definitely different".
- In *Alphabet Soup,* Priya also resents being "pre-judged" and discriminated against for being brown. Moreover, her rejection of some American values makes her feel at odds with the country she lives in. All are "legal aliens": although they are Americans lawfully, they are not considered as such by other Americans. It affects the way they view themselves.
- Aisha Harris's situation is different since she is not bilingual. But she also questions her identity because of other people. As she is regularly asked: "where are you from?" she understands defining herself as black American is not sufficient.

II. Identity crisis and sense of belonging?

- Aisha Harris becomes aware "identifying as black and African-American interchangeably" is wrong. Despite her father's attempt "to reestablish the lineal connection" between his black American daughter and her African roots, she cannot feel African-American because she does not "truly have access to both cultures". Her link with Africa is loose and remote. Her ancestors were slaves and no records were kept. She chooses black American. This shift stresses she experiences an identity crisis. So does Priya: she blames her father for "moving to America all those years ago" because she deems materialism corrupts her. She thus rejects her American identity.
- The teacher's mistakes and the pupils' puzzled faces show Jin is probably the only Chinese-American in the class. Though he wishes to integrate, his introduction prevents him from blending in: it stresses he is culturally different and does not belong there. *Legal Alien* also emphasizes hyphenated Americans cannot fit in as they are "on the fringes of both worlds", that is to say in an in-between state.

Adding hyphens to words that do not have any ("bi-cultural, bi-lingual") stresses the gap between hyphenated Americans and other people from either their native country or the USA.

■ Biculturalism means "discomfort" for hyphenated Americans as the two sides of their identity are separated by **the hyphen which characterizes them.**

> **CONSEIL**
> La synthèse suit les règles de présentation de la dissertation. Mais pour la synthèse vous devez toujours rester objectif. Attention à **ne pas donner votre avis** personnel.

III. Redefining one's identity: resolution?

■ Jin and the persona of *Legal Alien* **suffer from their fractured identity** and look for a solution from within. While Jin may find one by getting rid of "the scent of his old home", a metaphor for his Chinese upbringing and culture, the poet claims the symmetrical duality of biculturalism is the precondition of being whole. Her experience unravels in a 22-line sentence in one breath to prove that perpetual oscillation from one culture to the other is trivial.

■ On the other hand, Priya and Aisha Harris' resolutions **involve a trip abroad.** Aisha's touristic experience to Kenya makes her acknowledge her "kinship" with Africans and understand a "slice of African culture for herself". It helps her redefine herself and assert: "where I'm from is America–who I am is a black American", which includes the loss of her African heritage and sharing the culture and history of all Americans from African descent. Priya decides to go to India to reconnect with her roots as, for her, "assimilation is a betrayal of your skin". She views India as the place she can bond with, providing her "strength", making her proud of her skin.

■ Although they opt for totally different solutions, all try to redefine their fractured selves so as to **get rid of the never-ending in-between state** they endure.

Conclusion

Biculturalism is not a piece of cake: all documents stress how it affects everyday life and leads to a deep identity crisis. Whether those hyphenated Americans look for a solution within themselves or by going to the country of their ancestors, they try to redefine themselves so as to come to terms with their bicultural identity.

9 Traduction en français

« L'assimilation, c'est trahir ses racines, expliqua / exposa Priya à son père.
– Comment peux-tu considérer que travailler dur et réussir, c'est trahir ses racines ?
– Réussir ? Certes, mais à quel prix et selon les règles de qui ? »
Son père passa en revue leur maison / considéra leur maison (cinq chambres, une piscine, un garage pour trois voitures) et se mit à sourire. « Je suis ravi que tu aies les moyens de tes opinions, dit-il.
– Ton erreur, affirma-t-elle, ça a été de t'installer en Amérique autrefois.
– Tu aurais préféré grandir en Inde ?
– Plus j'y pense… oui, répondit-elle. Il y a une force certaine à être basané dans un pays où tout le monde est basané.
– C'est-à-dire ? / Mais encore ? / À savoir ?
– Eh bien, regarde comment on nous traite ici / on est traité ici. »

Les épreuves du bac

4 Faire une synthèse de documents

Réussir la synthèse suppose de maîtriser les caractéristiques de tous types de documents et d'en rendre compte de façon objective, concise et ordonnée.

FICHES DE COURS

EXERCICES & SUJETS

CORRIGÉS

19 Analysing fiction

En bref *It is first necessary to consider the text globally: find out what is said and who about. Then you have to concentrate on the writer's choices so as to access to full understanding.*

I Global understanding

1 The characters and the setting

- When reading the extract for the first time, it is necessary to find out basic facts such as who does what and where and when it takes place. It is useful to pick up various clues.

Elements of the text	Interpretation
Pronouns and possessive determiners	Identify the character·s clearly
Adjectives	Analyse the characters' appearances and personalities as well as elements related to the setting
References to time and space	Determine the historical and geographical background

- Chronological and logical link words give clues as to the chain of events and key moments of the plot. It is thus useful to find out if the events are told according to the chronological order or if there are flashbacks or flashforwards.

2 The narrator and point of view

- It is necessary to identify the narrator who tells the story and from whose point of view the story is told so as to fully understand the narrative.

Questions about the narrator

- Is it a first or third-person narrative?
- Is the narrator one of the characters of the story or not?
- Are there different narrative voices?
- Is there an omnipotent narrator?

- The narrator's role and stance do affect what the narrative tells and the way it is told. For example with an omnipotent narrator, the reader knows more than the characters, whereas with an objective narrator, the reader knows as much as the characters.

II Detailed understanding

1 Language

- The use of language (whether formal, colloquial or use of slang), the tone (whether ironical, humorous or tragic...), the atmosphere (whether stressful, conflicting or quiet...) of the extract are equally important and help to understand the main theme·s.

- Figures of speech play the same role. Whether they stress similarity, repetition or contrast, they always contribute to spotting the key ideas, themes or features.

  *Frankenstein **or the modern Prometheus**,* by Mary Shelley

  (This full version of the title comprises an allusion to the ancient myth of Prometheus.)

- Focusing on how long the sentences are or the tenses used, leads to an in-depth understanding of the extract. For example, short sentences may be used to account for a character's stream of consciousness.

  Was it possible they heard not? Almighty God! – no, no! They heard! – they suspected! – they knew! – they were making a mockery of my horror! – this I thought, and this I think. *The Tell-Tale Heart*, by E. A. Poe

2 Unknown vocabulary

- You should not panic when there are words you do not understand. Use different strategies so as to deduce what they mean. First observe the word in context: look at the preceding and following words, consider the nature of the word (noun, adjective, adverb, verb...). It gives useful clues to guess its meaning.

- You can then consider word formation processes. → FICHE 31

zoOm

What to look for when annotating?

Here are some ideas. Use different colours to underline the text.

Structure	• simple or multi-clause sentences • paragraph: how it opens or closes • repeated words and phrases • order of ideas in the excerpt
Language	• use of formal or standard English, colloquialism or slang • literary devices • words with particular connotation
Characterisation and voice	• key element showing the development of characters • clues about the main voice • story told in first or third-person
Themes and ideas	any words or phrases that link to the main themes or a particular semantic field

20 Analysing poetry

En bref *Poetry may be quite baffling. It is based on a different use of language stressing both its beauty and musicality. In order to deal with a poem, it may prove useful to tackle the story it tells (even if it is not that obvious) and to analyse the various literary devices at stake so as to be able to grasp its meaning (especially when it is confusing).*

I Literal meaning

Poems may tell a story or focus on feelings or a particular object but can be confusing. The first step consists in identifying the subject and theme of the poem thanks to the following clues.

Analysing a poem

- The **author's** name, the **date**, the literary movement, the title if any and what it suggests.
- The **character·s**, the persona whose viewpoint is developed, the person whom the poem is addressed if any.
- The **place·s**, real or imaginary, their characteristics and roles.
- If **objects** are included, the way they are presented and the role they play.

II Poetic language

Poetry is based on a different use of words, based on their suggestive powers and musical patterns. Impressions, suggestions and connotations are at the core of it.

1 Playing with layout and structure

It is necessary to pay attention to the visual aspect of the poem, so as to determine its general structure: the number of stanzas, of lines, of dashes and gaps. It will help analyse the effect and meaning of the layout.

A sonnet	A fourteen-line lyric poem in iambic pentameter. There are two different forms of sonnet: • **Shakespearean sonnet** = 3 quatrains rhyming ababbcbccdcd + one couplet rhyming ee; • **Petrarchan sonnet** = one octet (8 lines = 2 quatrains) + one sestet (6 lines = 2 tercets).
Free verse poem	No regular metrical pattern.
A visual poem	The lines are organized so as to form a shape which often evokes the topic of the poem.

2 | Playing with rhythm and sounds

- One of the key features of English verse is rhythm. It is indeed based on metrical patterns which are defined by the arrangement of stresses and their frequency of repetition per line.
- Poetry is organized by the division of each line into feet (= metric unit). Each foot is composed of two or three syllables with at least one stressed syllable. The most common metrical pattern is the **iambic** pentameter (iamb x 5).

  So fair – and foul – a day – I have – not seen.
  (*Macbeth*, Act 1, sc 3)

> **INFO**
> • **iamb**: unstressed syllable + stressed one, da-DUM: *beware*
> • **trochee**: stressed syllable + unstressed one, DUM-da: *garden*

- Rhythm is essential to creating the atmosphere of the poem. Any variation in the metrical pattern is significant. The musical effect of poetry also comes from other devices which enable to draw parallels or to contrast words: rhymes, alliterations, assonances, consonances, onomatopoeia...

Types of rhymes	
Couplet rhymes	aa, bb, cc (couplet = 2 lines)
Alternate rhymes	abab
Enclosing rhymes	abba
Eye rhyme	eat / great

zoOm

Playing with words

- Poets tend to invent a **new link between words**, thus creating new meanings and showing the world from a new angle thanks to these elements. Analysing all those features of the poem enables to access its inner meaning.

Unexpected associations	the air that shudders **black with snow** (Snow is white, meaning purity, innocence but here black conveys an idea of ill omen, announcing death.)
Figures of speech	They can establish an unusual relationship between two worlds through similes: comparisons, metaphors, personification, anaphora, oxymoron, chiasmus. the merciless iced east winds that knife us (personification)
Lexical fields and imagery	They stress the crucial elements. The stress may be laid on sensations thanks to a particular treatment of the five senses. **Watching**, we **hear** the mad gusts tugging on the wire. Like **twitching agonies** of men among its brambles. (different senses: sight, hearing, touch)

- All examples come from *Exposure* by Wilfried Owen.

→ Read the full poem: bit.ly/PbacAngTle_WOwen

21 Analysing drama

En bref *Drama is oral by nature. There is a close link between: the stage, the audience and the text. That's why you have to bear in mind that it is written for the purpose of being performed on stage, so visualising the scene while studying it may prove beneficial.*

I Studying plays: the text and its structure

- Plays are specific, with a **primary text** (the main body of the play spoken by the characters) and **secondary texts** (all the texts "surrounding" the main text): title, dramatis personae (*liste des personnages*), scene descriptions, stage directions (*didascalies*) for acting and speaking. The secondary texts provide with clues about the atmosphere, action or information about the characters' appearance or their tone of voice.

  [Inverness. A room in Macbeth's castle]
  Enter Lady Macbeth, reading a letter.
  LADY M.: They met me in the day of success...

- Plays are usually divided into a number of **acts** (five in Greek tragedies or in Shakespeare's plays) divided into **scenes**. First, situate the passage in the play: is it an exposition scene introducing who, what, when, where and why? Is it a scene helping the action to develop or part of the final denouement?

II Main characteristic features

1 Characters

Drama is centred on characters, who can be defined by the language they use. To study them determine:

Their status	Main or secondary characters, static or dynamic characters. Dynamic characters go through some sort of change while static characters do not evolve.
Their type	Stock characters representing specific stereotypes (a fool, a scheming villain...), always think about adjectives to describe their personality.

2 How is information conveyed?

- Define **who is speaking**, to whom, what about? In dialogues, determining the way speaking time is allocated helps understand whose perspective is adopted. How long are the lines? You must also differentiate **a monologue** (long speech delivered by one character), **a soliloquy** (long speech a character recite to himself) and an **aside** (a character speaking to the audience only).

- Study who is leading the conversation. Find out if some characters' views are expressed more clearly than others'. And finally, don't forget to study the silence which can be eloquent.

3 | Dramatic irony

- How much information is given can have different effects on the viewers and this must be taken into account. The discrepancy between the audience's and characters' knowledge of some information can lead to dramatic irony. Thus, duplicities or puns can be understood by the audience while the characters are ignorant and thus lack sufficient insight.
- For instance, in *Romeo and Juliet*, the audience knows that Juliet is only asleep – not dead – but Romeo does not, and he kills himself.
- Lack of necessary information can also lead to surprises for the audience, and this is often used in comedies to resolve confusions and mixed-up identities.

4 | Traditional features

- Poetry enjoyed its heyday (*apogée*) during the Elizabethan era (1558-1603), that's why the iambic pentameter → FICHE 20 was greatly used by William Shakespeare or Christopher Marlowe in their plays. But blank verse or even prose were also commonly used. For example, characters may use prose in informal situations but verse in more formal ones.
- The use of a chorus was also frequent, for example in *Henry V* by Shakespeare. They were characters not taking part in the actions of the play but commenting on the events or giving information to the audience.

zoOm

Prologue spoken by a chorus

Extract from *Romeo and Juliet*'s prologue written in sonnet. The audience is told what is about to happen: despite true love, an ill-fated couple ("star-crossed") won't escape their fate and will die.

> Two households, both alike in dignity,
> In fair Verona, where we lay our scene, (...)
> From forth the fatal loins of these two foes
> A pair of star-cross'd lovers take their life
> Whose misadventur'd piteous overthrows
> Doth with their death bury their parents' strife.
> The fearful passage of their death-mark'd love,
> And the continuance of their parents' rage, (...)
> Is now the two hours' traffic of our stage; (...)
> What here shall miss, our toil shall strive to mend.

- (yellow) Semantic fields of death, fate and fighting
- (blue) The audience is invited to feel sympathetic towards the protagonists
- (green) The audience is reminded that what is following is a play

22 Analysing non-fiction

En bref *Non-fiction can be divided into several types of texts which all aim at influencing, convincing, persuading or defending a point of view. When dealing with such a text, it is necessary to identify what sort of text it is, to analyse its structure and the linguistic devices used so as to understand the arguments which are developed.*

I Identifying the type of text

1 Press articles

- The sources, title and subtitles clearly point to press articles. Yet, there are different sorts of articles: leading articles (*articles de fond*), columns (*chroniques*), editorials (*éditoriaux*) or reviews (*critiques*).
- Even if they have a different structure, editorials, columns and reviews are subjective and express the opinion of the newspaper, the journalist or critic.

2 Critical texts and essays

- Philosophical or political essays and book or film reviews put arguments forward in using a clear structure: arguments and examples are carefully and gradually organised so as to back up a particular thesis.
- Formal language is used: long, often complex, sentences and specific vocabulary or imagery. Being able to pick up simple sentences helps to understand the text.

> **INFO**
> A **simple sentence** is composed of the elements that are absolutely necessary to grab its meaning: subject, verb, complement.

II Identifying the structure

1 Argumentation

- The main sequence in an argumentative text is composed of:
  - an introduction: it presents the theme or issue and what is at stake;
  - a body with arguments: it presents and defends the thesis: arguments, examples, references, testimonies, quotations, comparisons, anecdotes, precisions, refutation, counter-arguments;
  - a conclusion: it rephrases the thesis, sums up the justification and gives the final position.
- The first sentence of each paragraph always gives key information which is then further developed.

  Most people have no idea how advanced the technology has become: now faces can be tracked from half a mile away thanks to software called Intelligence Pedestrian Surveillance.

2 Arguments and examples

The writer proves his·her thesis thanks to arguments: the **substantive reasons** that justify it to convince the readers. Arguments have a general scope while examples deal with particular instances and illustrate arguments; they prove how relevant arguments are with a real case.

> It takes a lot of courage to whistleblowers to reveal sensitive information. (general scope) After revealing international spying by the NSA, Edward Snowden fled to Hong Kong then to Moscow in order not to be jailed. (particular instance)

III Being familiar with characteristics

1 Link words

Link words (conversely, obviously, besides...) are used to **relate** these arguments and examples. They establish logical connections between the ideas that are developed: cause, consequence, explanation, illustration, listing, comparison, contrast, compromising, conclusion... That's why it is necessary to pick them out.

2 Abstract vocabulary and figures of speech

- Figures of speech are used to **give a forceful demonstration** whether to argue for or against a thesis. Comparisons and similes assert similarities in a positive or negative way. Hyperbole uses exaggeration for effect:

> Millions of school children every year... (in a speech against school uniforms)

- There are many abstract words linked to ideas, notions, feelings and emotions.

zoOm

How to detect the autor's opinion

Various devices can be used to give one's opinion.

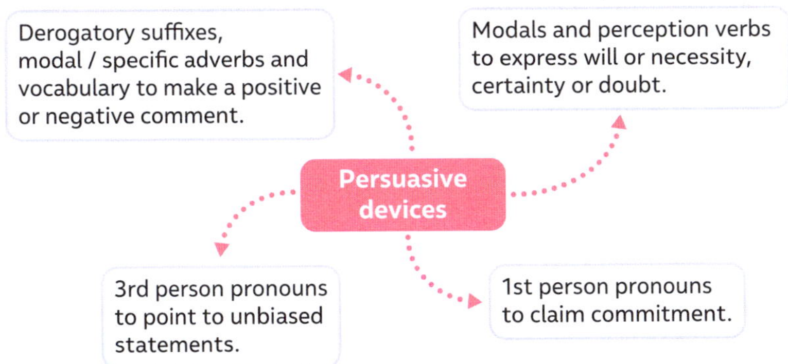

23 Analysing a picture

En bref *Pictures are meant to be looked at, to attract people's attention and to strike their imagination or to give a message. Their aim may be information, protest, ideology or personal representation. They require a specific language that needs deciphering so as to understand the artist's message. In order to decipher a picture, various steps are necessary.*

I Identifying and describing

1 Nature and origin

First identify the nature of the picture: it can be a painting, a photograph, a caricature, a cartoon or an ad (= an advert or advertisement), etc. Pick up all relevant information you can find: title, artist's name, date. If the picture is coupled with a **caption**, read it carefully, as it will help you define the main topic of the picture and its social and historical context.

INFO
caption: title or brief explanation or comment accompanying an illustration

2 Structure and content

- You can then pay attention to the layout *(disposition)*, then the setting and characters of your document.
- The layout is very important as it gives clues: the number of parts, the positioning (find out the focal point), the colours, light and shading, contrasts, the arrangements of volumes and shapes are key features that help understand the overall effect.
- Before describing what takes place, it is necessary to locate the scene so as to avoid misinterpreting the picture under study. When describing the characters always examine carefully their gestures, actions, body language, gaze and facial expressions.
- All these elements provide the general atmosphere conveyed by the picture.

II Construing and interpreting the intentions

1 Emotions and Symbols

- To analyse the artist's intentions, first concentrate on the emotions the picture arouses when you look at it. Try to describe what the image spontaneously evokes in you both positively and negatively, and what it is in the picture that makes you feel that way.

- Secondly identify the **symbolic** elements the picture contains. For example you can wonder if the doves represented in your picture stand for peace or if the colour red means danger, love or prohibition?

INFO

A **symbol** is a thing that stands for something else. Usually, it consists of a real object used to represent something more abstract or complex.

2 | The artist's goals

- To fully understand the artist's message, focus on the cultural, historical or artistic context as it may give further significant information. Relate them to all your findings so as to stress the artist's intentions.
- You should consider the purpose for which the image was created. Attempts to influence? To sell something? To denounce a situation? Who is the picture aimed at?

zoOm

How to situate the various elements in a picture

So as to describe what you can see as precisely as possible, use these prepositions.

24 La synthèse

En bref *La synthèse vise à mettre en lumière les relations entre les documents proposés et ne consiste pas en une énumération de thèmes communs. Cet exercice nécessite au préalable une analyse détaillée de chacun des documents.*

I Lire le dossier et rechercher les axes communs

1 Découvrir le dossier dans son ensemble

- Il faut prendre d'abord connaissance de la ou des **question·s** accompagnant les documents et en analyser tous les termes clés, afin d'identifier les différents éléments mis en tension qui justifient la question posée.
- Il faut ensuite identifier la nature des supports proposés, les indications périphériques (titres, sources et natures des documents) qui fournissent des éléments indispensables. Le but est ici d'avoir à l'esprit le **thème général du dossier**.

2 Procéder à l'analyse détaillée

- Il est indispensable de considérer chaque document dans sa **spécificité de forme et de contenu** avant de procéder à la synthèse proprement dite.
- Il faut procéder aux **premiers relevés** sur chaque document séparément à l'aide de surligneurs de différentes couleurs :

Relevés à effectuer

- Le **genre** et l'**idée générale**.
- La **manière** dont les éléments sont évoqués (tonalité du document).
- Les **détails pertinents** au regard de la question posée.
- Ce qui relève du **factuel** et de l'**implicite** (ce que l'auteur suggère au-delà des mots en utilisant un champ lexical ou des figures de style).

3 Effectuer l'étude comparative

- Il convient ensuite de procéder à une étude comparative des documents. Les consignes qui guident la synthèse permettent d'élaborer un **tableau synoptique**. Il donne une vue d'ensemble des différents repérages pour chaque document.

CONSEIL
Le **tableau synoptique** comprend autant de colonnes que de documents. On peut y ajouter une colonne supplémentaire intitulée : pistes de réflexion.

■ Le tableau doit faire apparaître les similarités ou les différences autour de notions ou de mots clés qui pourront relever aussi bien du contenu thématique (la folie, la ville, la pauvreté…) que de données structurelles (point de vue, mode de représentation…) ou esthétiques (gothique, pop'art…).

II Élaborer le plan et rédiger la synthèse

1 Construire le plan

Les différentes questions ou consignes du sujet correspondent aux différentes parties du plan. Celui-ci doit être clair et apporter une réponse à la question déterminée par l'analyse du sujet.

2 Rédiger la synthèse

■ L'introduction doit comporter une amorce, il faut présenter la thématique du dossier, caractériser rapidement chacun des documents, puis reformuler la problématique et annoncer les étapes de la démonstration, c'est-à-dire le plan.

■ Le développement doit suivre le plan. Il est constitué de paragraphes dans lesquels il faut avancer des arguments reposant sur les éléments repérés dans l'analyse. Le propos doit être cohérent, les causes et conséquences clairement établies. Chaque argument doit être illustré par un ou des exemple·s et s'appuyer sur les différents documents. Il faut veiller à soigner les transitions.

■ Le rôle de la conclusion est de répondre à la question présentée dans l'introduction. Elle dresse un bilan du devoir mais il faut éviter les redites et pour cela, veiller à reformuler les conclusions partielles énoncées à la fin de chaque partie. Attention, la conclusion ne doit jamais contenir d'idées nouvelles.

zoOm

Comment gérer son temps lors de l'épreuve (3 h 30)

Réflexion et brouillon	Lire les consignes, survoler le dossier Lire les questions et analyser les termes (15 min)
	Étudier attentivement chaque document (35-40 min)
	Étude comparative des textes Compléter le tableau synoptique (35-40 min)
Rédaction	Élaborer un plan détaillé au brouillon Rédiger l'introduction et une ébauche de conclusion (15 min)
	Rédiger le développement et la conclusion (45 min)
	Relire impérativement la synthèse (15 min)
Traduction	Prévoir 30-40 min

MÉMO VISUEL

Réussir l'épreuve

1 Analyser le sujet

Faites les repérages

- Identifiez la **thématique** du dossier et les différents **types de documents**.
- Repérez et analysez tous les **mots clés**.

Analysez les termes du sujet

- Mettez en **relation** les termes clés et la thématique du dossier.
- Formulez la **problématique** en tenant compte de tous les aspects et enjeux des différents documents.

4 Rédiger la synthèse

Rédigez l'introduction

Il ne faut omettre aucune de ses parties essentielles.

- Commencez par une **amorce**.
- Reformulez **le sujet**.
- Annoncez **le plan**.

Construisez le développement

- Mettez **en tension** les différents documents, en les citant tous et en dégageant clairement leurs structures et enjeux implicites.
- Distinguez plusieurs paragraphes chacun ayant au moins **deux sous-parties**.
- Soignez les **transitions** entre les différents éléments.

Rédigez la conclusion

Répondez clairement et précisément à la question formulée dans la problématique.

de synthèse

2 Faire le tableau synoptique

Il permet d'avoir une **vue synthétique de l'ensemble** des documents et de votre analyse.
C'est un outil indispensable, dans lequel on puise les différents arguments et exemples.

- Complétez le tableau avec des **exemples précis** et référencés.
- Constituez, à l'aide du tableau, le **plan détaillé**, avec les sous-parties.

3 Construire le plan

Il s'agit d'un travail de **reformulation** des pistes données dans le sujet.

- Analysez les **questions ou consignes** pour repérer les différentes parties qu'elles suggèrent.
- Formulez les **grandes parties du plan** qui en découle.

SE TESTER QUIZ

Vérifiez que vous avez bien compris les points clés des **fiches 19 à 24**.

1 Analyser un texte de fiction

→ FICHE 19

Cochez la voix narrative employée (1st or 3rd person narrative).

	1st	3rd
a. They surrounded me quickly and began to grab for my hand. "I'll kill you!" I threatened. (R. Wright, *Black Boy*)	☐	☐
b. Too stupefied to be curious myself, I fastened my door. (E. Brontë, *Wuthering Heights*)	☐	☐
c. Mrs. Dalloway said she would buy the flowers herself. (V. Woolf, *Mrs. Dalloway*)	☐	☐

2 Analyser un poème

→ FICHE 20

1. Associez chaque figure de style à sa définition.

a. alliteration •	• repetition of consonants
b. consonance •	• repetition of vowel sounds within a line
c. assonance •	• repetition of initial consonants

2. Vrai ou faux ? Cochez la case qui convient.

	V	F
a. A sonnet is a fifteen-line poem in iambic pentameter.	☐	☐
b. In a poem, each line is divided into metric units called iambic.	☐	☐
c. Rhythm takes part in creating the atmosphere.	☐	☐

3 Rédiger la synthèse

→ FICHE 24

Cochez les réponses correctes.

1. What is a synoptic chart and why should you use one?

☐ a. It's a chart which provides a general overview of the various documents.
☐ b. It's a chart which enables you to compare the documents easily.
☐ c. It's a chart which helps you identify the main topic of the key question.

2. What are the necessary elements to insert in your introduction?

☐ a. You should include a brief characterization of each document and announce your answer to the key question.
☐ b. You should include a thorough description of each document and announce the main parts of your outline.
☐ c. You should include a brief characterization of each document and announce the main parts of your outline.

3. What is the goal of your conclusion?

☐ a. To open up new perspectives.
☐ b. To make an assessment and answer the key question.
☐ c. To give your opinion on the documents.

S'ENTRAÎNER

4 Compléter un tableau synoptique

→ FICHE 24

Prenez connaissance des quatre documents (A, B, C, D) puis complétez le tableau.

Document A

This painting commemorates the forced relocation of Native American tribes imposed by the Indian Removal Act passed in 1830. They were removed from their native lands and taken to reservations.

Robert Lindneux, *Trail of tears*, 1942.

Document B

Prime Minister Kevin Rudd, addressed a National Apology to Australia's Indigenous peoples on February 13th 2008.

That today we honour the Indigenous peoples of this land, the oldest continuing cultures in human history.

We reflect on their past mistreatment.

We reflect in particular on the mistreatment of those who were Stolen Generations - this blemished chapter in our nation's history.

The time has now come for the nation to turn a new page in Australia's history by righting the wrongs of the past and so moving forward with confidence to the future.

We apologise for the laws and policies of successive Parliaments and governments that have inflicted profound grief, suffering and loss on these our fellow Australians.

We apologise especially for the removal of Aboriginal and Torres Strait Islander children from their families, their communities and their country.

For the pain, suffering and hurt of these Stolen Generations, their descendants and for their families left behind, we say sorry.

To the mothers and the fathers, the brothers and the sisters, for the breaking up of families and communities, we say sorry.

(...)

We the Parliament of Australia respectfully request that this apology be received in the spirit in which it is offered as part of the healing of the nation.

For the future we take heart; resolving that this new page in the history of our great continent can now be written.

We today take this first step by acknowledging the past and laying claim to a future that embraces all Australians.

A future where this Parliament resolves that the injustices of the past must never, never happen again.

(...)

A future based on mutual respect, mutual resolve and mutual responsibility.

A future where all Australians, whatever their origins, are truly equal partners, with equal opportunities and with an equal stake in shaping the next chapter in the history of this great country, Australia.

Kevin Rudd, National Apology to Australia's Indigenous peoples on February 13th 2008

Document C

This is a slam poem in response to Stephen Harper's 2008 "Statement of Apology to former students of Indian Residential schools[1]" in Canada.

I Know You're Sorry

All is not forgotten
When someone is forgiven
Words I say to soften up
The hardness that I'm livin'

I hate to say indifference
Is becoming my religion
But I haven't learned to pray
In ways to satisfy tradition

When I think about identity
I think about my language
And how my folks were taught
It would be to my advantage
To learn a foreign tongue
They could not foresee the
damage

Damn shame when it happens
you don't – see it til it passes
So where's all the support
For Anishinaabemowin[2]
classes?

Assimilation tactics
left no room for us to
practice.
And I really wish I could
adjust.
I really wish I could have just
Listened with my heart and
not my ego

I was fragile
Conditioned by the world
to think my culture wasn't
passed down
But I learned the generosity
It's in my genealogy

So fuck all the bureaucracy
And keep all your apologies

I know you're sorry but...
You're more lost than me
Your land's across the Ocean
and I'm right where I should
be.

I reckon this damn nation
Will force reconciliation
Down the throats of our
survivors
And the people it's displacing

I know you're sorry.

And now you call on me
To fix the broken hearts
Created by your policies

These are the things that I
think I know
I am but a leaf on a tree that
grows
With roots in the ground,
Like a seed that's sown
In the dirt of the earth
Is where I was born
And it's where I will return
When this journey ends
And I've earned what I have
learned

So tell me to get over it
I'm so fuckin' over it
Steal everything in sight
And teach me 'bout-private
ownership
Bleach everything you like
And preach me 'bout pride of
ownership
Leech my inherent rights
And tell me that I never
owned this shit

As generations pass
You'll act as if you never
noticed it
While there's kids committing
suicide
As a way out of the
hopelessness

I know you're sorry.

You say you're not to blame.
Fill your heart to brim with
guilt
But not an ounce of shame.
Break branches off our family
trees
And tell us times have
changed

But the focus of this genocide
At root remains intact,
So instead of killing Indian
kids
Why don't we kill this Indian
Act

Leonard Sumner, Slam poem in response to Stephen Harper's 2008
"Statement of Apology to former students of Indian Residential schools" in Canada,
Mannitoba, Canada, 2017, www.leonardsumner.com

À NOTER
Vous pouvez écouter le poème : bit.ly/PbacAngTle_LSummer

1. Residential schools were boarding schools where Indigenous children were forced to be educated away from their families and culture, in order to be assimilated into the dominant Canadian culture.
2. Anishinaabemowin is an indigenous language spoken by first Nation peoples in Canada (from southwestern Quebec, through Ontario, to Manitoba), and in the United States, (from Michigan to Wisconsin and Minnesota).

Document D

EXILED CHAGOS ISLANDERS DREAM OF RETURN

People evicted from former British colony hope new documentary Another Paradise *will reinforce UN calls for withdrawal*

The Chagos Islanders have had few victories in their long battle to return from British-enforced exile to their archipelago homeland in the Indian Ocean.

But small steps keep their campaign alive and it is hoped a documentary that will premiere on Saturday will exert pressure on the UK government to change its stance.

Britain's ongoing occupation of the islands was declared illegal in February in an "advisory opinion" by the international court of justice at The Hague. Last month, the UN general assembly showed overwhelming support for a motion setting a six-month deadline for a withdrawal from the Chagos Islands so the archipelago could be reunified with Mauritius.

Yet the islanders remain stuck in exile. After being evicted in the 60s and 70s, some Chagossians were given British passports in 2002; today, an estimated 3,000 second- and third-generation islanders live in Britain.

The film, *Another Paradise*, by Belgian director Olivier Magis, documents a community in Crawley, West Sussex, home to Britain's largest Chagossian population.

"The film serves to bring a shameful episode in Britain's post-colonial history out of the shadows," said Magis. "When you listen to the arguments of the British government in the past few years, everything is justified. Politicians talk about relocation, not deportation, without mentioning what really happened and the way it happened."

Sabrina Jean, 46, chair of the Chagos Refugee Group's UK branch, said she hoped the UN decision and the documentary, which will be shown at the Sheffield film festival on 8 and 10 June, would help: "We know the UN decision is not binding. I don't know yet what will happen but Chagossians will not sit down. We will fight for our rights."[1]

Karen McVeigh, "'I want to die on my native soil': exiled Chagos Islanders dream of return" in *The Guardian*, Friday 7 June 2019.

1. In November 2019, British Parliament refused to hand back the Chagos Islands.

Complétez le tableau avec les citations des différents documents.

Doc	The wrongs of the past	Legacy on next generations	Apologies = possible reconciliation?
A	Native Americans: sad faces, grey: Mass deportation → despair	1830s and 1942: suffering today due to lost heritage, grey storm → bleak future	
B	Australian Aborigines: forced assimilation → abduction of children: .... → despair:	• suffering today due to lost heritage and failure of forced assimilation → inequality: .... • aboriginal culture not fully accepted → fractured society	national apologies to make up for the past: .... and reunite a divided society .... → reconciliation: ....
C	First Nation peoples from Canada: • no land and white values example: .... • so denial of .... → forced assimilation .... • children taught in white schools → culture lost .... and language lost .... → shattered identity	• suffering today due to lost heritage and regrets: .... → desperate solution: .... • language still not taught .... Natives still ruled by the Indian Act • displacement still going on .... → fractured society	• response to national apologies: .... → pointless because nothing has changed: .... broken rhythm (final stressed syllables and enjambment) shows gap • apologies viewed as mistreatment .... → no reconciliation
D	Chagos Islanders: • forced exile in the 60s & 70s, some went to GB • UN decision supporting British withdrawal from the Chagos Islands and reunification with Mauritius → illegal occupation	• 2nd and 3rd generation islanders still stuck in exile → suffering due to lost heritage and land • "few victories and long battle to return home" : unsuccessful claim → fractured society	• colonialism now: "a shameful episode in Britain's post-colonial history" • ongoing fight: "we will fight for our rights"

OBJECTIF BAC

Vous avez 3 heures 30 pour réaliser la synthèse et faire la traduction proposée. C'est à vous de vous organiser pour produire l'ensemble dans le temps imparti.

5 Rédiger une introduction

Utilisez les mots suivants pour rédiger les quatre étapes de votre introduction.

a. Amorce : colonialism / economic and political control / territory / its inhabitants

b. Reformuler la problématique : colonialism / now over / topical issue/ English speaking countries / ?

c. Caractériser les documents : four documents / indigenous peoples/ different countries and periods / colonialism

d. Annoncer le plan de la synthèse : mistreatments / by white rulers/ creation of a fractured society/ possibility to bridge the gap?

6 Ébaucher une conclusion

Quelles idées devraient être développées dans votre conclusion? Choisissez la meilleure proposition.

☐ a. Acknowledging past mistakes is useless because the land is not given back. So forgiveness and reunification are impossible. As a result colonialism is not a thing of the past.

☐ b. Giving back the land is necessary because it helps acknowledging past mistakes and forgiveness and reunification become possible. Therefore colonialism is a thing of the past.

☐ c. Acknowledging past mistakes is necessary but first necessity to give back the land. If not forgiveness and reunification are impossible. Thus colonialism is not a thing of the past.

7 Rédiger la première partie

Remettez les paragraphes dans l'ordre logique.

→ .... / .... / .... / ....

a. Native American children were also taught in white schools and assimilated. As their "culture wasn't passed down" (l. 31-32) their descendants find it impossible to develop a sense of belonging.

b. In Australia, as Kevin Rudd states in his apology speech to the Aborigines, that policy meant the abduction of thousands of Aboriginal children, known as the "Stolen Generations" (l. 4-5). It led to the "breaking up of families and communities" (l. 17).

c. That loss of the land is also underlined in "I know you're Sorry" written by Leonard Sumner, an Anishinaabe poet, where the persona accuses the white settlers of stealing his land and depriving him of his native culture by imposing their values as they "steal everything in sight / And teach me 'bout private ownership" (l. 65-67). Denying these peoples their identity and culture was part of the rulers' policy of forced assimilation.

d. The Guardian's article and Robert Lindneux's painting, both focus on the mass deportation imposed on local populations. The exiles' sad faces stress how helpless they were. Indeed, the Native Americans had to give up their lands and nomadic lives while the Chagossians had to abandon "their archipelago homeland in the Indian Ocean" (l. 4-5).

8 Rédiger la deuxième partie

Rédigez les phrases en utilisant les références au tableau et les amorces.

a. Situation for the descendants today + example of doc. A

→ Although these mistreatments took place in the past, ...

b. Source of the difficulties today and impact on their everyday life in today's society + example doc. C

→ The loss of their heritage is still the core of the despair and grief experienced by many, who are unable to ...

c. Outcome of policies of forced assimilation + examples doc. B, C

→ These policies of assimilation have bred suffering, but to missed their goal ...

9 Construire une transition

Complétez avec les liens logiques qui conviennent : consequently, besides, thus, so as to

a. Transition 1 : Colonialism has .... deprived indigenous peoples of their ancestral land and denied them access to their culture and traditions in the long term.

b. Transition 2 : ...., nothing seems to have changed for these peoples. Their claims to their lands and their cultures were despised in the past, and are still not fully recognized today. ...., colonialism and forced assimilation have only managed to create a divided society.

10 Rédiger la troisième partie

Rédigez les trois paragraphes de cette partie en vous aidant du tableau.

a. National apologies (where? why? use doc. B & C)

b. Reaction / similar or different answer? (use doc. C & D)

c. Have apologies improved the situation? (use doc. C & D)

11 Conclure une synthèse

En vous basant sur votre réponse à l'exercice 6, rédigez votre conclusion.

CORRIGÉS

SE TESTER QUIZ

1 Analyser un texte de fiction

a. 1st • b. 1st • c. 3rd

2 Analyser un poème

1. a. repetition of initial consonants • b. repetition of consonants • c. repetition of vowel sounds within a line

2. a. Faux. A sonnet is a fourteen-line lyric poem in iambic pentameter. • b. Faux. Each line is divide into feet, it's a metric unit, each foot is composed of two or three syllables including at least one stressed syllable. • c. Vrai.

3 Rédiger la synthèse

1. a et b • 2. a et b • 3. a et c

S'ENTRAÎNER

4 Complétez un tableau synoptique

Doc	The wrongs of the past	Legacy on next generations	Apologies = possible reconciliation?
A	--	--	
B	Australian Aborigines: forced assimilation → abduction of children: "Breaking up of families and communities" (l. 17) → **despair:** "profound grief, suffering and loss" (l. 10)	• suffering today due to lost heritage and failure of forced assimilation → inequality: "A future where all Australians, (...), are truly equal partners, with equal opportunities" (l. 31) • aboriginal culture not fully accepted → **fractured society**	• national apologies to make up for the past: "this blemished chapter in our nation's history" + "acknowledging the past" (l. 23) and reunite a divided society "a future that embraces all Australians" (l. 24) → **reconciliation:** "healing of the nation" (l. 20)

Doc	The wrongs of the past	Legacy on next generations	Apologies = possible reconciliation?
C	First Nation peoples from Canada: • no land and white values example: "steal everything in sight / And teach me 'bout private ownership" (l. 65-67) • so denial of traditional way of life → forced assimilation "hopelessness" (l. 80) • children taught in white schools → culture lost "my culture wasn't passed down" (l. 31-32) and language lost "learn a foreign tongue" (l. 13) → **shattered identity**	• suffering today due to lost heritage, regrets: "And I really wish I could adjust" (l. 24-25) → desperate solution: "While there's kids committing suicide" (l. 77-78) • language still not taught "So where's the support / For Anishinaabemowin classes?" (l. 18-20) • Natives still ruled by he Indian Act • displacement still going on "And the people it's displacing" (l. 46) → **fractured society**	• response to national apologies: "I know you're sorry but ..." + "keep all your apologies" (l. 36) → pointless because nothing has changed: "But the focus of this genocide / At root remains intact" (l. 90-91) broken rhythm (final stressed syllables and enjambment) shows gap • apologies viewed as mistreatment: "I reckon this damn nation / Will force reconciliation / Down the throats of our survivors" (l. 42-45) → **no reconciliation**
D	--	--	--

OBJECTIF BAC

5 Rédiger une introduction

a. Colonialism involved economic and political control over a territory and its inhabitants.

b. But, now that it is over, is it a topical issue in English-speaking countries?

c. The four documents under study are about indigenous peoples from different countries and periods facing colonialism.

d. They highlight the mistreatment imposed by white rulers, resulting in the creation of a fractured society but also question the possibility to bridge such a gap.

6 Ébaucher une conclusion

Réponse c.

7 Rédiger la première partie

L'ordre logique est : d-c-b-a.

8 Rédiger la deuxième partie

a. ..., they still affect the descendants of all these peoples. The painting dating back to 1942 highlights that more than a century after their mass deportation their everyday life is still as bleak as the grey colours used by the artist. It seems that they are forever walking in stormy weather.

b. ..., "really wish (they) could adjust" (l. 24-25) are unable to adapt and therefore "there's kids committing suicide / As a way out of hopelessness..." (l. 77-80).

c. ...: the Aborigines are still not considered as true "equal partners" in 2008; the Native are still ruled by the "Indian Act" in Canada; the Chagossians "have had few victories in their long battle to return" home and they "remain stuck in exile".

9 Construire une transition

a. Native American children were also taught in white schools and assimilated. As their "culture wasn't passed down" (l. 31-32), their descendants found it impossible to develop a sense of belonging. Colonialism has thus deprived indigenous peoples of their ancestral land and denied them access to their culture and traditions in the long term.

b. Consequently, nothing seems to have changed for these peoples. Their claims to their lands and their cultures were despised in the past, and are still not fully recognized today. Besides, colonialism and forced assimilation have only managed to create a divided society.

10 Rédiger la troisième partie

a. Well aware of such damage, some governments (Australia, Canada) publicly apologised as an attempt to heal past wounds and bring a fractured country together. "By acknowledging the past and laying claim to a future that embraces all Australians", some politicians hope to erase "this blemish chapter in our nation's history" as Kevin Rudd says in his speech. His repetition of the pronoun "We" shows he recognizes former governments' responsibility. But is recognition enough? Can reconciliation be considered?

b. The poem can be read as a response to those apologies: "keep all your apologies / I know you're sorry but." Such apologies are worthless because they are not backed up with significant change "But the focus of this genocide / At root remains intact." The gap is obvious like the broken rhythm of the poem produced by enjambments and pauses induced by strongly stressed final words.

c. The article tends to answer similarly. This "shameful episode in Britain's post-colonial history" (l. 21-22) means Chagos Islanders are undergoing an ongoing illegal occupation. Saying sorry, as Kevin Rudd repeats, doesn't mean putting an end to any type of mistreatment "I reckon this damn nation / will force reconciliation / Down the throats of our survivors / And the people it's displacing." Long after the dreadful abuses were committed, indigenous populations remain in the same pernicious position.

11 Conclure une synthèse

Acknowledging past mistakes is necessary but, whatever the place, as long as these peoples' ancestral lands are not given back, their enduring suffering won't come to an end. That's why forgiveness may not be pondered on, and reunification may be impossible even after offering national apologies. As a consequence, colonialism is definitely not a thing of the past and the fight goes on for those people since, according to Leonard Sumner, "Your land's across the ocean and I'm right where I should be."

Synthèse intégrale :

Introduction

Colonialism involved economic and political control over a territory and its inhabitants. But, now that it is over, is it a topical issue in English speaking countries? The four documents under study are about indigenous peoples from different countries and periods facing colonialism. They highlight the mistreatment imposed by white rulers, resulting in the creation of a fractured society but also question the possibility to bridge such a gap.

I. The wrongs of the past / human rights abuses

- The article "*Exiled Chagos Islanders dream of return*" and Robert Lindneux's painting, *the Trail of Tears* both focus on the mass deportation imposed on local populations. The exiles' sad faces stress how helpless they were. Indeed, the Native Americans had to give up their lands and nomadic lives while the Chagossians had to abandon "their archipelago homeland in the Indian Ocean" (l. 4-5).
- That loss is also underlined in "I know you're Sorry" written by Leonard Sumner, an Anishinaabe poet, where the persona accuses the white settlers of stealing his land and depriving him of his native culture by imposing their values as they "steal everything in sight / And teach me 'bout private ownership" (l. 65-67). Denying these peoples their identity and culture was part of the rulers' policy of forced assimilation.
- In Australia, as Kevin Rudd states in his apology speech to the Aborigines, that policy meant the abduction of thousands of Aboriginal children, known as the "Stolen Generations" (l. 4-5). It led to the "breaking up of families and communities" (l. 17).
- Native American children were also taught in white schools and assimilated. As their "culture wasn't passed down" (l. 31-32), their descendants find it impossible to develop a sense of belonging. Colonialism has thus deprived indigenous peoples of their ancestral land and denied them access to their culture and traditions in the long term.

II. Aftereffects: mistreatments reverberated down next generations / legacy

- Although these mistreatments took place in the past, they still affect the descendants of all these peoples. The painting dating back to 1942 highlights that more than a century after their mass deportation their everyday life is still as bleak as the grey colours used by the artist. It seems that they are forever walking in stormy weather.

■ The loss of their heritage is still the core of the despair experienced by many, who "really wish (they) could adjust" (l. 24-25), are unable to adapt and therefore "there's kids committing suicide / As a way out of hopelessness..." (l. 77-80).

■ These policies of assimilation have bred suffering, but missed their goal: the Aborigines are still not considered as true "equal partners" in 2008; the Natives are still ruled by the "Indian Act" in Canada; the Chagossians "have had few victories in their long battle to return" home and they "remain stuck in exile."

■ Consequently, nothing seems to have changed for these peoples. Their claims to their lands and their cultures were despised in the past, and are still not fully recognized today. Besides, colonialism and forced assimilation have only managed to create a divided society.

III. Bridging the gap

■ Well aware of such damage, some governments (Australia, Canada) publicly apologised as an attempt to heal past wounds and bring a fractured country together. "By acknowledging the past and laying claim to a future that embraces all Australians", some politicians hope to erase "this blemish chapter in our nation's history" as Kevin Rudd says in his speech. His repetition of the pronoun "We" shows he recognizes former governments' responsibility. But is recognition enough? Can reconciliation be considered?

■ The poem can be read as a response to those apologies: "keep all your apologies / I know you're sorry but ..." Such apologies are worthless because they are not backed up with significant change "But the focus of this genocide / At root remains intact." The gap is obvious like the broken rhythm of the poem produced by enjambments and pauses induced by strongly stressed final words.

■ The article tends to answer similarly. This "shameful episode in Britain's post-colonial history" (l. 20-21) means Chagos Islanders are undergoing an ongoing illegal occupation. Saying sorry, as Kevin Rudd repeats, doesn't mean putting an end to any type of mistreatment "I reckon this damn nation / will force reconciliation / Down the throats of our survivors / And the people it's displacing." Long after the dreadful abuses were committed, indigenous populations remain in the same pernicious position.

Conclusion

Acknowledging past mistakes is necessary but, whatever the place, as long as these peoples' ancestral lands are not given back, their enduring suffering won't come to an end. That's why forgiveness may not be pondered on, and reunification may be impossible even after offering national apologies.

As a consequence, colonialism is definitely not a thing of the past and the fight goes on for those people since, according to Leonard Sumner, "**Your land's across the ocean and I'm right where I should be.**"

CONSEIL

Teminer par une phrase particulièrement frappante, style punchline, est un plus !

5 Améliorer son expression

Pour rédiger une synthèse de bonne qualité, vous devrez acquérir un vocabulaire et des structures grammaticales élaborées qui mettront en évidence la qualité de votre anglais.

25 Parler d'un document

En bref *La présentation et la référence aux documents du dossier sont cruciaux dans votre synthèse. Vous devez utiliser un vocabulaire précis qui montrera l'attention portée aux différents documents ainsi que des tournures de phrases élégantes qui vous permettront de vous démarquer du reste des candidats.*

I Connaître les mots utiles pour décrire un document

1 Utiliser un vocabulaire précis pour présenter un document

■ Lorsque vous analysez un document, vous devez utiliser les termes appropriés. Ne vous contentez pas de parler du « document ».

Œuvres littéraires	a novel, a novella, a short story, a poem, a play, a song…
Œuvres visuelles	a photograph, a picture, a painting, an engraving, an ad, a film poster, a film, a video, a recording, a cartoon, a building, a sculpture…
Œuvres d'idées	a speech, an essay, an article…

✗ The set of documents is composed of document A by W. Lewis, document B by R. Aldington and document D by J. Heller.

✔ The set of documents is composed of a **painting** by W. Lewis, two **poems** by R. Aldington and an extract from the **novel** *Catch-22*.

■ L'auteur d'un document doit également être présenté de façon précise (*novelist*, *playwright*, *singer*, *director*, *cartoonist*, etc.).

CONSEIL
Pour exprimer l'origine d'une œuvre ou d'un extrait, il faut utiliser *by* + nom de l'auteur et *from* + nom de l'œuvre.

2 Utiliser les verbes adéquats pour analyser un document

Traiter un thème	deal with, mention, be about…
Illustrer	exemplify, serve as an example, illustrate…
Représenter une idée	epitomise, embody, represent…
Mettre l'accent	highlight, underline, point out, stress…
Reprendre une idée	mirror, reflect…

The excerpt **deals with** self-representation in art and **highlights** the role of social media. The journalist **stresses** the way in which Sherman's work **reflects** the selfie culture.

II Éviter les répétitions

1 Utiliser les bons pronoms

- Vous pouvez utiliser des **pronoms personnels** pour remplacer un sujet. Il faut cependant faire attention au genre du référent (*he*, *she* ou *it*).

  Though a critically acclaimed novel, J.D. Salinger's *The Catcher in the Rye* (1951) was met with outrage when **it** was published in the United States.

CONSEIL
Attention à ne pas doubler votre sujet en utilisant un nom et un pronom : *The article Ø was written in 2017.*

- Les **pronoms démonstratifs** (*this* ou *that*) permettent de reprendre des paroles déjà prononcées.

  Aristotle coined the term catharsis to refer to the purging of one's emotions through art. **This** was first used to discuss tragedy.

2 Utiliser d'autres procédés de reprise

D'autres **expressions pronominales** peuvent être utilisées : *the latter* (pour reprendre le dernier élément mentionné) et *the former* (pour reprendre le premier élément mentionné).

Owen's point of view contrasts with the position of other poets like Thomas Hardy. **The latter** poets glorified the war and introduced soldiers as heroes dedicating themselves to their country.

zoom

Citer le titre d'une œuvre en anglais

Les 3 règles clés

Pour un roman, une pièce de théâtre, un film, une peinture, un journal, le titre doit être souligné.
<u>Interstellar</u>
<u>The New York Times</u>

Tous les mots doivent commencer par une majuscule (sauf les articles et les prépositions).
<u>Romeo and Juliet</u>
<u>Leaves of Grass</u>

Pour un poème, une nouvelle, un discours, il faut utiliser des guillemets anglais.
"Bombardment"
"I Have a Dream"

26 Bien organiser sa synthèse

En bref *L'organisation de votre synthèse est primordiale. Une synthèse s'organise en plusieurs parties qui s'articulent grâce à des connecteurs logiques qui mettront en avant la pertinence de votre réflexion.*

I Rédiger une introduction

1 Présenter les documents

L'introduction consiste à présenter les documents que vous allez analyser dans votre synthèse. C'est également le moment opportun pour **introduire le thème** de la synthèse afin de montrer à votre correcteur que vous êtes conscient·e des tenants et aboutissants du dossier.

> The **documents under study** are a painting by Millais, *Ophelia*, a poem by Keats, "Ode to a Nightingale" and the lyrics from Pharell Williams's song, "Happy". They deal with the representation of emotions in art.

2 Introduire la problématique

Après avoir présenté les documents, vous devez introduire votre problématique. Elle est le **fil conducteur** de votre synthèse : chaque partie de votre analyse devra être en lien avec elle. Vous ne devez pas vous en éloigner.

> I shall therefore **focus on** the artistic depiction of the soldiers' gradual annihilation in the documents.

3 Annoncer le plan

L'annonce de votre plan est primordiale car celui-ci est la **colonne vertébrale de votre analyse**. Votre correcteur doit savoir où votre analyse va vous mener.

> I will **first** focus on the depiction of the material damage. I shall **then** turn to the processes used to dehumanise the soldiers. **Lastly**, I will analyse how the artists intertwine death and madness.

CONSEIL
Sautez des lignes et faites des alinéas à chaque étape de votre introduction pour la rendre claire et montrer que vous avez réfléchi à son organisation.

II Faire progresser son propos

1 Organiser son paragraphe

Lorsque vous rédigez le corps de votre synthèse, chaque paragraphe doit contenir une idée principale étayée par un exemple tiré des documents. Vous pouvez utiliser un **connecteur** en début de paragraphe pour signaler que vous introduisez une nouvelle idée.

Introduire une idée	first, firstly, first of all, to begin with…
Ajouter des idées	secondly, thirdly… then, next, afterwards, after that… what is more, moreover…
Conclure un paragraphe	lastly, finally…

Then, in "Alphabet Soup", Priya also resents being "pre-judged" and discriminated against for being brown. **Moreover**, her rejection of some American values makes her feel at odds with the country she lives in.

2 Ménager les transitions

Il est nécessaire d'écrire une courte transition lorsque vous passez à une autre partie. En quelques lignes, vous devez **résumer l'idée principale** de la partie que vous venez de rédiger pour ensuite expliquer en quoi votre deuxième partie est la **suite logique de votre analyse**.

III Rédiger une conclusion

Dans votre conclusion, vous devez **résumer les idées principales de votre analyse**, soit chaque grande partie. Introduisez votre conclusion avec une expression telle que *to conclude, as a conclusion* ou *in a nutshell*…

To conclude, the documents **first** highlight their own artificiality: the reader's attention is drawn to staging and sublimation. **Then**, references to religious figures in all the documents lead to a sanctification of the image. **Lastly**, the documents lead us to criticise our image-obsessed society.

CONSEIL
Rédigez votre conclusion en même temps que votre introduction. Vous n'aurez plus qu'à la copier en fin d'épreuve si vous manquez de temps.

zoOm

Les 3 règles clés pour faire une citation

1. Utilisez les guillemets anglais : "I have a dream that one day …"
S'il y a des guillemets dans la citation, ils deviennent des apostrophes simples.
"'That's some catch, that 'Catch-22', he observed."

2. Situez votre citation en précisant le numéro de ligne (l. 1) ou le paragraphe :
in the fourth parahraph / stanza

3. Choisissez des citations courtes et écrivez-les en entier.

27 Utiliser le connecteur logique approprié

En bref *La synthèse est un exercice d'argumentation où vous devrez mettre en évidence les liens entre les documents et démontrer la pertinence de vos analyses par l'utilisation de connecteurs logiques.*

I Exprimer l'opposition ou la similarité

1 Comparer les documents

Les documents du corpus expriment une idée commune, ou s'opposent entre eux. Au brouillon, vous pouvez faire un tableau pour faire apparaître ces similarités et ces oppositions.

2 Utiliser le connecteur logique approprié

- Après avoir identifié les liens entre les documents, vous devrez utiliser les connecteurs logiques appropriés pour les exprimer.

  All three documents present us with "dramatically staged self-portraits". **Both** documents use self-representation to present the viewer with a seemingly well-constructed image of the self. Sherman's Instagram account, **on the other hand,** deconstructs the idea of the self as Instagram might promote it.

- Plusieurs connecteurs vous permettront de mettre l'accent notamment sur la similarité et l'opposition.

Similarité	all three + N, both, likewise, similarly…
Opposition	although, in contrast with, in opposition to, contrary to, unlike, while, whereas, on the one hand, on the other hand…

II Exprimer la cause ou la conséquence

1 Identifier les liens de causalité

Quand on analyse une œuvre d'art, on est amené à élucider son fonctionnement interne. On est conduit à établir les liens de cause et de conséquence existant entre ce qui est explicitement dit dans le document et ce que l'on en déduit.

2 Utiliser le connecteur logique approprié

- Une fois les liens identifiés, vous pouvez au choix mettre l'accent sur la cause.

  In "Song of Myself", Whitman emphasizes sexuality **as** he introduces himself as "sensual".

Sherman criticizes the selfie culture **given that** she uses distorted selfies instead of presenting the viewer with a glamourized version of herself.

- Ou sur la **conséquence**.

  Whitman's and Bowery's self-portraits present their viewer or reader with a shocking representation of themselves, **thus** emphasizing sexuality.
  Sherman's "distorted selfies" build on a contemporary trend **in order to** criticize the "staging" of oneself on social media in the late 2010s.

- Voici les principaux connecteurs possibles.

Cause	because, as, for, due to, on account of, given that, insofar as...
Conséquence	so (that), thus, in consequence, therefore, hence, consequently, in order to, that is why, to this end...

III Exprimer la finalité

1 Identifier les effets

Analyser un document, c'est mettre en évidence **les effets qu'il produit** sur le lecteur ou le spectateur. Vous devrez montrer au correcteur que vous les avez relevés et expliquer leur fonction.

2 Choisir le bon connecteur

Une fois que vous avez identifié le but servi par un procédé littéraire, introduisez-le par un connecteur exprimant **la finalité** : *to*, *in order to*, *so as to*.

Leigh Bowery uses drag **to** catch the viewer's attention
In "Song of myself", Walt Whitman directly addresses the reader **in order to** involve them from the very beginning of the poem.
Cindy Sherman distorts her image **so as to** question female identity.

zoom

Exprimer la condition

L'utilisation de connecteurs exprimant la condition vous permet également de nuancer votre propos en exprimant une hypothèse.

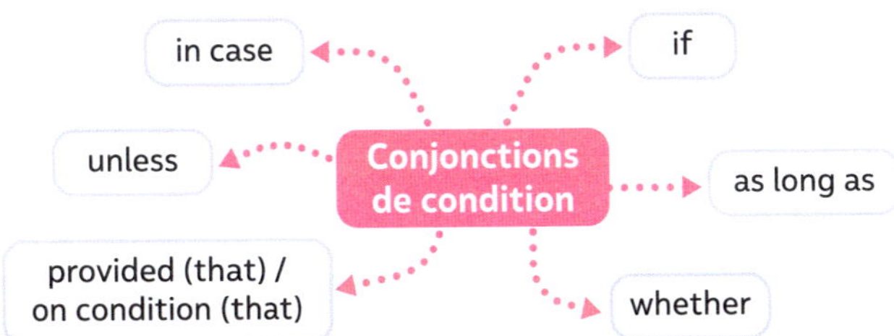

28 Utiliser le temps et l'aspect qui conviennent

En bref *L'anglais différencie les temps (le présent et le prétérit) des aspects (be + -ing et have + -en). Les temps et les aspects n'expriment pas la même chose bien que les aspects puissent être associés au présent ou au prétérit. Lors de la rédaction de la synthèse, souvenez-vous que vous êtes évalués sur la qualité et la richesse de la langue.*

I Choisir le temps approprié

L'anglais n'a que deux temps grammaticaux : le présent et le prétérit.

1 S'exprimer au présent

On utilise le présent simple pour parler de quelque chose qui est **toujours vrai au moment où l'on parle**. C'est le temps que vous utiliserez le plus.

> In "Happy", Pharell Williams **conveys** happiness through the lyrics and music.

À NOTER
À la 3e personne, le verbe prend un *-s*. Attention, les verbes qui finissent en *-s*, *-sh*, *-ch*, *-x* prennent un *e* avant le *s*. Les verbes finissant par *-y* prennent *-ies* : *finishes / carries.*

2 Utiliser le prétérit

Le prétérit permet de parler d'une **action passée décorrélée du présent**. Il implique une rupture entre le passé et le présent. Le prétérit est le temps principal du récit au passé.

> Her link with Africa is loose and remote. Her ancestors **were** slaves and no records **were** kept.

Ici, on adopte le point de vue d'un personnage dont on évoque l'histoire. On évoque un fait appartenant au passé, ce qui explique le passage du présent au prétérit.

3 Renvoyer à l'avenir

S'il n'existe pas de futur en anglais, le renvoi à l'avenir s'opère de deux façons.

- Avec le ***modal will***.

On utilise le modal *will* suivi d'un verbe à l'infinitif pour parler d'un événement dont on est certain qu'il aura lieu à l'avenir. C'est cette forme que vous utiliserez pour annoncer votre plan.

> First, I **will** show the importance of the expression of emotions in this set of documents. Then, I **will** analyze how the viewer, or reader is made to share the emotions expressed in the documents.

- Avec ***be going to***.

On utilise le semi-modal *be going to* pour parler d'une action programmée dans un futur relativement proche. *Be going to* relève d'un registre de langue peu formel, qu'il ne faut pas utiliser à l'écrit.

II Choisir l'aspect approprié

Les aspects expriment un point de vue sur l'action, ils permettent de la décrire dans son déroulement ou bien de faire le lien entre un moment du passé et le moment dont on parle.

1 Décrire une action dans son déroulement : *be* + *-ing*

Pour décrire une action en cours de déroulement, on utilise *be* conjugué au présent ou au prétérit, et le verbe à la forme *-ing*.

In the cartoon, the pupils' puzzled faces stress that he probably is the only Chinese-American in the class. They **are** all **staring** at him.

Dans le cadre de la description d'image, la forme *be* + *-ing* s'impose le plus souvent. L'action est en train de se dérouler, donc on met le verbe *stare* à la forme *-ing* et on conjugue *be* au présent.

2 Faire le lien entre deux moments : *have* + participe passé

Quand on parle d'une action en lien avec un événement antérieur, on conjugue *have* au présent ou au prétérit (le moment repère) et on met le verbe au participe passé (le moment passé).

Human emotions **have** long **constituted** the very material of art.

Ici, on parle d'histoire de l'art : il faut faire le lien entre un moment du passé où les émotions constituaient le matériau de l'art et le moment du présent où c'est toujours le cas.

zoOm

Rester cohérent

Lorsque vous utilisez un aspect, c'est toujours l'auxiliaire qui porte la marque du temps, et non pas le verbe infinitif.

Si votre phrase est au présent, attention à utiliser les aspects au présent.

The article **deals** with the fashion industry
✔ and it has been well received by designers.
✗ and it had been well received by designers.

Si votre phrase est au prétérit, attention à utiliser les aspects au prétérit.

The author **wrote** about the importance of selfies
✔ but he was being sarcastic.
✗ but he is beeing sarcastic.

29 Améliorer sa rédaction

En bref *Si la variété de votre lexique est importante, votre maîtrise de la grammaire et de la syntaxe l'est aussi. L'élégance de votre propos passe également par l'emploi de différentes structures grammaticales.*

I Varier la construction de ses phrases

1 Utiliser le passif

La structure passive permet de mettre en valeur celui qui subit l'action (l'objet) plutôt que celui qui agit (le sujet).

✗ The author published the novel in 1922.

✔ The novel **was published** in 1922.

2 Employer une proposition relative

Elles vous permettent d'**apporter des précisions** et d'**étoffer** votre propos. Elles sont introduites par des pronoms relatifs qui dépendent du type d'antécédent et de la fonction du pronom relatif. Elles peuvent être des **incises**.

À NOTER
Les **incises** (propositions entre virgules) permettent d'ajouter des informations ponctuelles sans interrompre la logique de votre analyse.

	Antécédent humain	Antécédent non humain
Sujet	The character, **who** is central... The character, **that** is central...	The novel, **which** deals with war... The novel, **that** deals with war...
Complément direct	The writer **that** you admire... The writer **Ø** you admire...	The book **that** you read... The book **Ø** you read...
Complément indirect	The writer **Ø** I told you about...	The poem **Ø** I told you about...
Complément de nom	Virginia Woolf **whose** work is discussed...	The article **whose** title...

3 Souligner une corrélation

Les termes corrélatifs forment une paire et doivent être utilisés dans la même phrase. Ils permettent de proposer deux idées et de les **associer** ou de les **opposer** : *neither... nor... ; either... or... ; whether... or... ; both... and... ; the more... the less...*

Whether those hyphenated Americans look for a solution within themselves **or** by going to the country of their ancestors, they try to redefine themselves.

II Nuancer ses propos : le *hedging*

1 Utiliser des modaux

■ Le ***hedging*** consiste à **atténuer une affirmation** pour laisser la place à une autre interprétation potentielle. Les anglophones sont moins assertifs que les francophones dans leurs analyses de documents.

CONSEIL
Le ***hedging*** peut s'utiliser avec des verbes comme *appear*, *seem*, *tend*, *suggest*... qui sont moins assertifs que d'autres (*assert*, *indicate*...).

■ Les modaux permettent de jouer sur le **degré de certitude** :

Modal	Certitude	Exemple
Can	très assertif	The text can be considered as an example of...
May	assertif	The painting may embody the artist's wish to...
Could	peu assertif	The article could illustrate the issue of...
Might	très peu assertif	The speech might reflect the speaker's view on....

→ Regardez une courte vidéo sur le *hedging* : bit.ly/PbacAngTle_hedging

2 Utiliser des adjectifs et des adverbes

Certains adjectifs et adverbes permettent d'**atténuer vos assertions**.

Adjectifs	possible, probable, conceivable, arguable...
Adverbes	likely, unlikely, possibly, often, usually, rarely, generally, typically...

The author's name clearly suggests that he is himself Chinese-American so the graphic novel is **likely** to give a genuine vision of biculturalism.

zoOm

Se relire : les 4 règles clés

La relecture est capitale : vous devez vous assurer de la fluidité et de la correction orthographique et syntaxique de votre devoir.

1. Ajoutez des connecteurs logiques.
2. Ajoutez des modaux ou adverbes pour atténuer votre analyse.
3. Employez des pronoms ou des synonymes lorsque vous remarquez des répétitions.
4. Corrigez les fautes d'inattention.

MÉMO VISUEL

Lorsque vous évoquez les documents dont le dossier se compose, veillez :
- à utiliser le **vocabulaire** approprié,
- à utiliser des **procédés** de reprise,
- à **bien citer** les titres et les passages des documents.

1 Parler d'un document

Améliorer

5 Améliorer sa rédaction

Vous devez utiliser des **structures variées** qui vous permettent d'approfondir votre réflexion et de nuancer votre propos :
- le **passif**,
- les **propositions relatives**,
- le ***hedging***.

Votre synthèse doit suivre plusieurs **étapes-clés** :
- **l'introduction** présente les documents, la problématique et le plan,
- **le développement** comporte plusieurs parties et des transitions logiques,
- **la conclusion** résume les idées principales du développement.

2 Bien organiser sa synthèse

son expression

Votre développement doit témoigner d'un **effort d'argumentation** :
- **distinguez plusieurs étapes** dans votre analyse,
- **utilisez** les connecteurs logiques appropriés pour faire **progresser votre démonstration**.

3 Utiliser le bon connecteur logique

4 Utiliser le temps et l'aspect qui conviennent

Quand vous conjuguez un **verbe**, interrogez-vous sur :
- l'emploi du **temps** (présent ou prétérit),
- l'emploi de **l'aspect** (*be* + *-ing*, *have* + participe passé).

La rédaction de la synthèse se fait principalement au présent simple mais vous devez aussi maîtriser les autres formes verbales.

SE TESTER QUIZ

Vérifiez que vous avez bien compris les points clés des **fiches 25 à 29**.

1 Parler d'un document

→ FICHE 25

Associez chaque œuvre à sa nature.

a. *Who's afraid of Virginia Woolf?* •	• Mural
b. *On the Road* •	• Poem
c. *Bright Star* •	• Novel
d. "In Memoriam A.A.H." •	• Film
e. "I remember when all of this was trees" •	• Play

2 Utiliser le connecteur logique approprié

→ FICHE 27

Classez les connecteurs logiques dans la colonne qui convient.
thus, in consequence, because, therefore, hence, as, for, consequently, due to, in order to, that is why, to this end, on account of, given that

Cause	Consequence

3 Utiliser le temps et l'aspect qui conviennent

→ FICHE 28

1. Quel temps et quel aspect doit-on utiliser pour décrire l'action montrée dans une image ?

☐ **a.** le présent et *have* + participe passé
☐ **b.** le prétérit et *be* + *-ing* ☐ **c.** le présent et *be* + *-ing*

2. Cochez le temps et l'aspect utilisés.

a. The earth is being torn under the soldiers' feet.
☐ présent ☐ prétérit ☐ *be* + *-ing* ☐ *have* + participe passé
b. There have always been the same types and forms of migration triggered by the same circumstances and reasons.
☐ présent ☐ prétérit ☐ *be* + *-ing* ☐ *have* + participe passé
c. Artists such as Vivian Maier chose to bear witness to their era by capturing it through photography.
☐ présent ☐ prétérit ☐ *be* + *-ing* ☐ *have* + participe passé

4 Améliorer sa rédaction

→ FICHE 29

Laquelle de ces phrases est un exemple de *hedging* ?

☐ **a.** The artist criticises traditional forms of art by creating a new form.
☐ **b.** The artist may criticise traditional forms of art by possibly creating a new form.
☐ **c.** The artist fails to discuss the political context.

S'ENTRAÎNER

5 Éviter les répétitions

→ FICHE 25

Réécrivez chaque paragraphe en évitant les répétitions.

a. The photograph shows Bowery in drag. The photograph shows the use of make-up, jewellery and the hat he is wearing. The photograph shows that Bowery plays with gender.

b. The painting talks about love while the novel talks about mourning. The article talks about reconciliation.

6 Repérer la similarité et l'opposition

→ FICHE 27

Soulignez les connecteurs logiques dans la couleur qui convient.

similarité	opposition

Both Lord Alfred Tennyson and Pharrell Williams used emotions as the subject matter of one of their works. However, the two artists are from different eras, and produced art using different mediums. Tennyson was a renowned poet from the 19th century whereas Williams is a contemporary pop singer. Unlike Pharell Williams, Alfred Tennyson's "In Memoriam A.A.H." focuses on grief.

7 Exprimer la cause et la conséquence

→ FICHE 27

À partir de chaque ligne du tableau, formez deux phrases : la première exprimant la cause, la seconde la conséquence.

Cause	Conséquence
a. Aïsha Harris does not "truly have access to both cultures".	Aïsha Harris cannot feel African-American.
b. In *Catch 22*, the soldiers' names are rarely used.	The soldiers' personalities are erased.
c. Through transvestism, Grayson Perry distorts his own image.	He questions the traditional representation of a gendered self.

8 Les propositions relatives

→ FICHE 29

Utilisez le pronom relatif qui convient.

1. Although the meaning of tattoos may be confusing, there is a growing interest in that tradition .... is now promoted.

2. The use of free verse .... conveys a conversational tone shows the perpetual oscillating movement between those two symmetrical aspects of biculturalism is trivial.

3. He was an English naturalist .... decided to embark on a five-year voyage around the world on the HMS Beagle to study exotic wildlife.

OBJECTIF BAC

9 Corriger un extrait de synthèse

Lisez cet extrait de la copie d'un élève et surlignez les différents types d'erreurs en utilisant le code couleur ci-dessous.

Erreurs de temps	Répétitions
Connecteurs	Citations

Ode to a Nightingale by Keats, Ophelia by Millais, and the lyrics of Happy by Pharell Williams talk about the emotions in art. The documents have shown different emotions and they have used different artistic genres. In Ode to a Nightingale, the author is sad, in happy, the songwriter emphasizes positive emotions and in Ophelia, the artist uses a sad subject-matter to talk about death. So the documents represent intense emotions in different ways. In Happy the lyrics and the music make the audience share the feelings expressed by the song and invite the listener to be happy like Pharrel Williams: « Clap along if you feel that happiness is the truth ». In the picture, the artist uses dim colours to show the death of Ophelia. But in Ode to a Nightingale, the artist talks about the happiness of the bird « being too happy in thine happiness » but the poem is about death too « for many a time I have been half in love with easeful Death ». So we have a contrast between Ophelia and Happy, and Ode to a Nightingale show the two sides together.

CORRIGÉS

SE TESTER QUIZ

1 Parler d'un document

a. play • b. novel • c. film • d. poem • e. mural

2 Utiliser le connecteur logique approprié

Cause : because, as, due to, on account of, given that
Conséquence : thus, in consequence, therefore, hence, consequently, in order to, that is why, to this end

3 Utiliser le temps et l'aspect qui conviennent

1. Réponse c. Une image montre souvent une action en déroulement. On utilisera *be* + *-ing* pour en rendre compte. L'affirmation est vraie au moment où l'on parle, on doit donc utiliser le présent.

2. a. présent / *be* + *-ing* • b. présent / *have* + participle passé • c. prétérit

4 Améliorer sa rédaction

Réponse b. The artist **may** criticise traditional forms of art by **possibly** creating a new form.

S'ENTRAÎNER

5 Éviter les répétitions

a. The photograph represents Bowery in drag. It highlights the use of make-up, jewellery and the hat he is wearing. The picture underlines the fact that Bowery plays with gender.

b. The painting deals with the theme of love while the novel discusses mourning. The article mentions reconciliation.

6 Repérer la similarité et l'opposition

Both Lord Alfred Tennyson and Pharrell Williams used emotions as the subject matter of one of their works. However, the two artists are from different eras, and produced art using different mediums. Tennyson was a renowned poet from the 19th century whereas Williams is a contemporary pop singer. Unlike Pharell Williams, Alfred Tennyson's "In Memoriam A.A.H" focuses on grief.

7 Exprimer la cause et la conséquence

Cause: a. Aïsha Harris cannot feel American because she does not "truly have access to both cultures". • b. The soldiers' personalities are erased as their names are rarely used. • c. Grayson Perry questions the traditional representation of a gendered self since he distorts his image through transvestism.

Conséquence: a. Aïsha Harris does not have access to both cultures. Consequently, she cannot feel African-American. • b. In *Catch 22*, the soldiers' names are rarely used. Therefore, the soldiers' personalities are erased. • c. Through transvestism, Grayson Perry distorts his own image, thus questioning the traditional representation of a gendered self.

8 Les propositions relatives

1. Although the meaning of tattoos may be confusing, there is a growing interest in that tradition which / that is now promoted.
2. The use of free verse which / that conveys a conversational tone shows the perpetual oscillating movement between those two symmetrical aspects of biculturalism is trivial.
3. He was an English naturalist who / that decided to embark on a five-year voyage around the world on the HMS Beagle to study exotic wildlife.

OBJECTIF BAC

9 Corriger un extrait de synthèse

Ode to a nightingale by Keats, Ophelia by Millais, and the lyrics of Happy by Pharell Williams talk about emotions in art. The documents have shown different emotions and they have used different artistic genres. In Ophelia, the topic of death is sad, in Happy, the songwriter talks about positive emotions and in Ode to a Nightingale, the artist uses joy and sadness. So the documents represent intense emotions in different ways. In Happy the lyrics and the music make the audience share the feelings expressed by the song and invite the listener to be happy like Pharrel Williams: « Clap along if you feel that happiness is the truth ». In the picture, the artist uses dim colours to show the death of Ophelia. But in Ode to a Nightingale, the artist talks about the happiness of the bird shared by the speaker « being too happy in thine happiness » but the poem is about death too « for many a time I have been half in love with easeful Death ». So we have a contrast between Ophelia and Happy, and Ode to a Nightingale show the two sides.

Erreurs de temps	Répétitions
Connecteurs	Citations

CONSEIL

Bien qu'un travail d'analyse soit présent dans cet extrait, les idées de l'élève sont affectées par une langue trop pauvre qui ne permet pas de mettre en valeur les repérages pertinents de ce premier paragraphe.

Extrait corrigé :

"Ode to a Nightingale" by Keats, Ophelia by Millais, and the lyrics of Happy by Pharell Williams all highlight the importance of emotions in artistic expression. The three documents use different artistic media in order to represent rather intense emotions. While the painting stresses sadness, the song emphasizes positive emotions, as the poem links the two constrasting feelings together. The intensity of the emotions represented in these three documents is quite striking. Pharell Williams's lyrics invite the audience to share the feelings expressed by the songwriter 'Clap along if you feel that happiness is the truth'. In the painting, Millais uses dim colours to frame Ophelia's death. However, in "Ode to a Nightingale", the artist brings happiness to the fore "being too happy in thine happiness" in a poem which ultimately deals with mortality "for many a time I have been half in love with easeful Death". Thus the emotions which appear in Ophelia and Happy, are both present in "Ode to a Nightingale".

6 Traduire un texte en français

Nul besoin d'être un expert en linguistique pour réussir la traduction : il faut considérer l'exercice comme un puzzle où chaque pièce trouve sa place.

* Il fallait traduire : Angela a commencé à pleurer à cause de la douleur, elle doit encore se remettre de sa blessure.

30 Se lancer dans une traduction

En bref *La version (traduction de l'anglais vers le français) a un double objectif : tester la compréhension de la langue source mais aussi la maîtrise de la langue cible. Cet exercice rigoureux requiert une démarche spécifique en plusieurs étapes.*

I La procédure générale

1 Aborder le passage

- Relisez le texte puis le passage à traduire attentivement. La version doit faire suite à l'analyse du texte qui a permis une **compréhension fine** de celui-ci et de ses caractéristiques.
- Repérez la nature du passage, les personnages, leurs rapports, le ou les lieux, l'époque, les événements, **le point de vue, le ton et le niveau de langue**.
- Délimitez les **unités de sens** avant de commencer.

To the European settlers the whole province looked like a barbaric place inhabited by appalling terrifying bloodthirsty savages.

MOT CLÉ
unité de sens : mots ou groupes de mots pertinents du point de vue de la syntaxe et du lexique

2 Traduire

Il s'agit de **restituer le sens d'origine** en tenant compte des spécificités linguistiques et culturelles de chacune des deux langues ainsi que des particularités inhérentes au texte d'origine.

Les 4 règles clés

1. **Commencez par une traduction littérale** (ou mot à mot).
2. **Affinez la traduction** en utilisant des procédés de traduction → FICHE 33, en cherchant à trouver le mot juste, l'expression adéquate.
3. **Rédigez dans un français authentique** rendant compte du style et du niveau de langue du texte source.
4. **Relisez la traduction** pour vous assurer que le sens du message est clair en français. Puis relisez parallèlement le texte en anglais et la traduction pour vérifier que rien n'a été omis.

II Conseils pratiques

1 **Évitez le recours systématique au dictionnaire** : il est parfois possible de surmonter autrement les difficultés lexicales. → FICHE 32

2 **Évitez le mot à mot systématique** : il faut tenir compte de l'ordre canonique de la phrase et respecter les conventions propres à chaque langue : succession des adjectifs, place des compléments circonstanciels…

Caitrin is a beautiful talented Irish woman who lives with her grumpy old uncle in a tiny flat in London.

✗ Caitrin est une femme irlandaise belle et talentueuse qui vit avec son oncle vieux et grincheux dans un minuscule appartement à Londres.

✔ Caitrin est une belle Irlandaise talentueuse qui vit à Londres dans un minuscule appartement avec son vieil oncle grincheux.

3 **Tenez compte des conventions d'écriture** : emploi des signes de ponctuation, utilisation des majuscules ou minuscules.

She loves Irish music, just like her secret admirer.

✔ Elle adore la musique irlandaise, tout comme son admirateur secret.

4 **Veillez à la correction de la langue cible**, grammaire, syntaxe et orthographe : une langue fautive est sanctionnée même si la traduction montre une bonne compréhension du texte. Attention au passé simple notamment et au franglais !

The old lady in charge of her musical education was so exhausted and downhearted that she sat down on the damp grass.

✗ La vieille femme en charge de [*franglais*] son éducation musicale était si épuisé et découragé [*accord*] qu'elle s'asseya [*conjugaison, barbarisme*] sur l'herbe mouillée.

zoom

Sur traduire ou sous-traduire

Il convient de vérifier que l'on n'a ni **sous-traduit** ni au contraire **sur-traduit**, ce qui induirait soit une perte au niveau du message soit une interprétation plutôt qu'une traduction.

Sous-traduction	Sur-traduction

She fondly dwelt on her long-gone glorious past as a grand piano player: her career had taken her abroad to Switzerland, Italy and Russia.

→ Elle pensait tendrement à son ancienne carrière glorieuse de grande pianiste : ses tournées de plus en plus nombreuses l'avaient amenée à se produire partout en Europe, en particulier en Suisse, en Italie et en Russie.

31 Traduire le lexique

En bref *La version est un exercice de précision qui requiert une bonne connaissance du lexique dans les deux langues. Face à des mots ou expressions inconnus, il faut adopter plusieurs stratégies pour aboutir à une traduction juste : inférer dans un premier temps le sens des mots puis utiliser le dictionnaire unilingue.*

I Utiliser le contexte et ses connaissances

■ Utiliser le contexte et identifier la nature et la fonction grammaticale du lexique inconnu permet d'accéder au sens et d'envisager une première traduction qu'il faudra peut-être affiner selon le cas.

She has become a grumpy old lady and she keeps complaining and whining, she finds fault in everything.

La forme et place du mot indiquent qu'il s'agit d'un verbe et le contexte permet d'en déduire qu'il a un sens proche de *complain* (se plaindre) donc ***whine*** **= geindre**.

■ Pour avoir un solide bagage lexical, il convient d'apprendre le lexique régulièrement et d'enrichir ses connaissances de synonymes et expressions idiomatiques. Cela permet ensuite de repérer rapidement les mots transparents et les faux amis.

sympathetic → compréhensif, compatissant
eventually → finalement
sensible → raisonnable

II Analyser la formation des mots

■ Maîtriser les procédés de dérivation, c'est-à-dire comment se forment les mots, permet de retrouver le mot racine et ainsi en fonction des **suffixes et préfixes** repérés d'inférer le sens des mots inconnus.

carefully = *care* + *ful* = adj. + *ly* = adv.
→ soigneusement
unfriendly = *un* + *friend* + *ly* = adj.
→ hostile, déplaisant

À NOTER
L'ajout de **préfixes** a un impact direct sur le sens du mot alors que l'ajout de **suffixes** change aussi la catégorie grammaticale de celui-ci.

■ Connaître la règle de composition permet de traduire convenablement les mots composés, qu'il s'agisse d'adjectifs ou de noms. En anglais, le mot qui se trouve en dernière position porte le sens principal et le mot qui se trouve en position initiale permet de préciser celui-ci.

homemade → fait maison
horserace → course de chevaux
racehorse → cheval de course

zoOm

Comment utiliser le dictionnaire unilingue ?

Yet, Caitrin couldn't blame her for the old lady's mood swings and **helplessness** reminded her of her beloved uncle.

- Identifier la **racine du mot** ou du moins débarrasser le mot inconnu de tous les marqueurs grammaticaux tels que la marque du pluriel ou encore les modifications verbales (V-*ing*, prétérit, participe passé) permet de rendre la recherche plus efficace.

helplessness = ***help*** + *less* + *ness*

- Déterminer la **catégorie grammaticale** des mots inconnus permet de s'intéresser directement à la bonne proposition dans le cas où un même mot aurait plusieurs natures.

helplessness = nom car génitif + suffixe *ness*. *Help* est ici un nom en raison des règles de dérivation : le suffixe *less* se rajoute toujours à un nom pour former un adjectif.

help² *n* **1** [U] the act of helping; AID; ASSISTANCE: *You're not (of) much help to me just sitting there. | You gave me a lot of help* **2** [C (*to*)] something or somebody that helps: *You're a good help to me. | The new fire is a great help* **3** [U *nonassertive*] a way of avoiding (esp. in the phr. **no help for it**) **4** [C] a person, esp. female, who is employed to do some of someone else's housework: *The new help left after a week* **5** [P] esp. AmE workers, esp. female house servants: *The help are demanding higher wages* **6** **Help!** **a** Please bring help, I'm in danger **b** (an expression of surprise and inability to act) **7** **Help Wanted** (a sign offering employment)

(bleu) Polysémie : lire l'article en entier avant de choisir la définition qui convient en fonction du contexte.

(orange) Caractéristiques : repérer si le mot est dénombrable (C pour *countable*) ou indénombrable (U pour *uncountable*) et où il est utilisé (AmE = American English par exemple). Le niveau de langue peut être précisé (fml = soutenu, lit = littéraire, coll / infml = familier, sl = argot).

(rouge) Synonymes : ils peuvent permettre de trouver une traduction adéquate.

(vert) Exemples : ils orientent la compréhension et la traduction en donnant un contexte d'emploi.

(rose) Expressions idiomatiques ou collocations, expressions figées.

→ Pourtant, Caitrin ne pouvait lui en vouloir car les sautes d'humeur et la **détresse** de la vieille dame lui rappelaient son oncle bien aimé.

32 Utiliser les procédés de traduction

En bref *Toute traduction passe nécessairement par l'utilisation de procédés de traduction. Il convient de distinguer les procédés directs de traduction qui sont utilisés lors du premier jet et les procédés indirects de traduction qui permettent d'affiner ce premier jet souvent maladroit, fautif, voire incompréhensible en français.*

I Les procédés directs

1 La traduction littérale

Il s'agit d'une version **mot à mot** qui reste au plus près du texte de départ, avec le minimum de transformations nécessaires. Si la structure syntaxique de l'énoncé est la même dans les deux langues, on se concentre sur le lexique, les déterminants et les formes verbales.

She had only found fault with her right from the start and it had nothing to do with her so-called gift: she disapproved of both her manners and her gait.

Elle ne lui avait trouvé que des défauts dès le début et cela n'avait rien à voir avec son soi-disant don : elle n'approuvait ni ses manières ni son allure.

2 L'emprunt

- L'emprunt consiste à **importer dans la langue cible** un mot ou une expression de la langue source, c'est-à-dire à employer le mot ou l'expression tels quels.
- Il permet de combler une lacune culturelle ou linguistique :

  coroner, sheriff, pub

- de faire « couleur locale » :

  hello (pour *bonjour*)

- de simplifier la phrase, notamment quand le terme est plus court :

  hacker, sniper

3 Le calque

- Les calques sont toujours fautifs, même si certains sont entrés dans l'usage. Il s'agit de traduire un mot ou une expression en important dans la langue cible une structure propre à la langue source dans le cas du **calque de structure** :

  for discussion → pour discussion

  (maintenant acceptable en français, même si c'est un anglicisme – à la place de *pour qu'on en discute*, qui est la tournure naturelle en français)

- Le calque permet aussi d'employer en français un mot ou une expression qui n'a pas le même sens que celui recherché dans le cas du **calque d'expression** :

  Secretary of State → secrétaire d'État (au lieu de *ministre des Affaires Étrangères*)

II Les procédés indirects

1 La transposition

- La transposition consiste à opérer un **changement de catégorie grammaticale** sans modifier le message, par exemple du nom au verbe, de l'adjectif au nom.

  Diamonds are Forever → Les diamants sont éternels

- Il y a deux cas particuliers de transposition : l'**étoffement** quand on remplace un mot par plusieurs, et le **chassé-croisé** quand on permute les éléments signifiants.

  He ran across the lawn. → Il a traversé la pelouse en courant.

2 L'équivalence

- L'équivalence consiste à **remplacer une formule plus ou moins figée de la langue source par une autre**, équivalente dans la langue cible. Elle est utilisée pour les expressions idiomatiques, proverbes, panneaux de signalisation, etc.

  You're welcome. (en réponse à *thank you*) → Il n'y a pas de quoi. / Avec plaisir.

- **L'adaptation** est rattachée à une situation donnée ou à l'arrière-plan culturel. On s'en sert pour les dialectes, jargons, jeux de mots notamment mais aussi pour les unités de mesure : **gallons** → litres avec conversion.

3 La modulation

Elle opère un **changement de point de vue** au niveau du message. Mais le sens global est conservé. Ce changement engendre un glissement d'ordre lexical ou d'ordre grammatical.

English spoken. → Ici, on parle anglais.
quite maliciously → non sans malice

zoOm

Les titres de films

Ils doivent être accrocheurs et peuvent parfois être très surprenants.

Mot à mot	The Fifth Element	Le cinquième élément
Transposition	How The West Was Won	La conquête de l'Ouest
Modulation	Harry Potter and the Philosopher's Stone	Harry Potter à l'école des sorciers
Modulation et transposition	The Bourne Identity Despicable Me	La mémoire dans la peau Moi, moche et méchant
Équivalence	As Good As It Gets	Pour le meilleur et pour le pire
Choix d'un titre anglais	The Hangover The Boat That Rocked	Very Bad Trip Good Morning England

33 Résoudre les problèmes de traduction

En bref *Les problèmes de traduction sont liés aux spécificités des deux systèmes linguistiques. Les problèmes d'ordre grammatical concernent les groupes nominal et verbal ainsi que la phrase et nécessitent la combinaison de plusieurs procédés de traduction.*

I Les groupes nominal et verbal

1 Le groupe nominal

- L'emploi des **déterminants** (article et possessifs) peut être différent.
  John's mother is *a* nurse. → La mère de John est Ø infirmière.
  He had *his* hands in *his* pockets. → Il avait *les* mains dans *les* poches.
- Les **adjectifs** décrivant une relation entre le nom et un autre élément ne se traduisent pas par des adjectifs.
  medical student → un étudiant *en médecine*

Il faut faire attention à **l'ordre des adjectifs** dans le cas d'une suite d'adjectifs.

À NOTER
Avant un nom, *beau, joli, bon* précèdent les autres adjectifs. **Après un nom**, les adjectifs les plus généraux sont devant et les participes passés à la fin.

- Les **pronoms possessifs** peuvent se traduire par des adjectifs possessifs.
  John is a friend of *mine*. → John est un de *mes* amis.

2 Le groupe verbal

Structure grammaticale	Choix de traduction	Exemple
Passif	Voix active	He *was given* a book yesterday. → *On lui a donné* un livre hier.
Modaux	Adverbes	He *must* be a policeman. → Il est *très certainement* policier.
Formes en *-ing*	Différemment selon leur fonction	Smoking is forbidden. → Il est interdit de fumer. I am warning you. → C'est un avertissement.
Reprise par auxiliaire	Sans l'auxiliaire	I didn't know about it. *Did you?* → Je n'étais pas au courant. *Et toi* ?
Verbes à particules	Dans certains cas, chassé-croisé	I'll ride back. → Je rentrerai en vélo. He ran into the room. → Il est entré dans la pièce en courant.

II La phrase

1 Structures causatives et résultatives

■ Les structures causatives sont traduites selon le même modèle : il s'agit de faire faire quelque chose, éventuellement à quelqu'un.

He made me do it again. → Il m'a fait recommencer.

He had the wall painted. → Il a fait peindre le mur.

■ Les structures résultatives mettent l'accent sur le résultat d'une action et le moyen pour l'obtenir. Elles s'utilisent donc pour convaincre ou persuader.

He talked him out of driving. → Il l'a dissuadé de conduire.

Elles peuvent aussi signifier un changement de lieu ou d'état.

I ate myself sick. → Je me suis rendu malade à force de manger.

2 Relatives et ponctuation

■ Dans le cas d'une **relative déterminative**, donc sans virgule, il peut être nécessaire d'étoffer.

My sister who is a model is in Leeds. → Celle de mes sœurs qui est mannequin est à Leeds.

■ Dans le cas d'une **relative non déterminative**, on traduit en respectant la ponctuation.

My sister, who is a model, is in Leeds.
→ Ma sœur, qui est mannequin, est à Leeds.

À NOTER
Une **relative déterminative** est nécessaire à la compréhension du message alors qu'une **relative non déterminative** apporte une information supplémentaire.

zoom

Comprendre la correction de sa copie

En plus des erreurs de français, les erreurs de traduction sont signalées par des termes précis.

Type d'erreur	Définition
Faux-sens	Prendre un mot pour un autre. Traduire *sparrow* (moineau) par « hirondelle ».
Contresens	Faux-sens aggravé montrant que l'on n'a pas compris. Traduire *sparrow* par « flèche » (*arrow*).
Non-sens	Texte absurde ou incohérent dans la langue cible.
Omission	Oubli considéré comme un abandon ou un refus de traduire face à la difficulté.
Syntaxe	Erreurs dans l'ordre des mots, pouvant aller jusqu'à construire une syntaxe qui n'existe pas dans la langue.
Temps	Erreur de choix de temps ou de forme verbale.

MÉMO VISUEL

Réussir l'exercice

1 Aborder la traduction

Lancez-vous dans l'exercice

- Commencez par **lire le texte** attentivement, **l'analyser** et repérer les unités de sens.
- Proposez une **première traduction littérale**, mot à mot, donc très proche du texte même si elle ne sonne pas tout à fait juste.

Traduisez le lexique

- **Inférez le sens des mots** grâce à leur fonction grammaticale, leur nature, leur formation.
- Utilisez ensuite le **dictionnaire unilingue** pour trouver le mot juste si nécessaire.

3 Relire sa copie

Relisez le texte en français

- Assurez-vous que le **message** est clair et immédiatement compréhensible.
- Vérifiez que la **langue** est correcte, qu'il s'agisse de l'orthographe, de la grammaire et de la structure ou de la ponctuation.

Utilisez les procédés de traduction

- Améliorez la traduction littérale pour proposer **un texte qui sonne juste** en français.
- Effectuez les transformations nécessaires :
  - changez certaines catégories grammaticales sans modifier le message originel en utilisant **la transposition** ;
  - modifiez le point de vue en utilisant **la modulation** ;
  - remplacez les expressions typiques en utilisant **l'équivalence**.

2 Affiner la traduction

de traduction

Résolvez les difficultés

- Prenez en considération les **spécificités des deux langues** pour proposer la traduction la plus authentique possible.
- Prêtez attention aux **temps des verbes**, à l'ordre des mots et au **niveau de langue**.

Relisez la traduction et le texte original en même temps

- Assurez-vous que vous avez **réellement traduit** et pas interprété le texte original, que vous n'avez ni sous-traduit ni sur-traduit.
- Vérifiez que vous avez **respecté le texte source**, que vous n'avez pas modifié le message originel et qu'il n'y a aucune omission.

SE TESTER QUIZ

Vérifiez que vous avez bien compris les points clés des **fiches 30 à 33**.

1 Traduire le lexique

→ FICHE 31

1. Associez chaque expression au niveau de langue employé.

a. annoyed	•	• formal
b. pissed off	•	• informal / colloquial
c. discontented	•	• vulgar / slang

2. Traduisez par des procédés de dérivation et selon la composition.

a. an unforgettable creepy-crawler → ....

b. admiring cave-drawings → ....

c. unobtainable records → ....

2 Utiliser les procédés de traduction

→ FICHE 32

1. Vrai ou faux ? Cochez la case qui convient.	**V**	**F**
a. On traduit les verbes à particules à l'aide du chassé-croisé.	☐	☐
b. La transposition opère un changement de point de vue.	☐	☐
c. On ne peut traduire les expressions idiomatiques et les proverbes.	☐	☐
d. Le calque est une traduction littérale souvent fautive.	☐	☐

3 Résoudre les problèmes de traduction

→ FICHE 33

Cochez la traduction qui convient.

1. Paula's and John's parents talked them into staying.

☐ a. Les parents de Paula et ceux de John leur ont parlé de rester.
☐ b. Les parents de Paula et ceux de John les ont convaincus de rester.
☐ c. Les parents de Paula et John les ont persuadés de rester.

2. He had had different jobs. And all the while he studied and read.

☐ a. Il avait eu divers emplois. Et, durant tout ce temps, il étudiait et il lisait.
☐ b. Il avait eu divers emplois. Et, durant tout ce temps, il étudia et il lut.
☐ c. Il eut divers emplois. Et, durant tout ce temps, il avait étudié et lu.

3. He had been on the sofa ever since he'd lost his job.

☐ a. Il avait passé son temps sur le canapé depuis qu'il avait perdu son travail.
☐ b. Il passait son temps sur le canapé depuis qu'il avait perdu son travail.
☐ c. Il a passé son temps sur le canapé depuis qu'il a perdu son travail.

S'ENTRAÎNER

4 La transposition et la modulation

Traduisez les phrases suivantes en utilisant les procédés adaptés.

a. He eventually staggered into the lifeboat.

→ ....

b. Her nails definitely need attention.

→ ....

c. A Mrs Jones keeps ringing.

→ ....

d. Don't forget to pick up the kids!

→ ....

CONSEIL
N'hésitez pas à utiliser plusieurs procédés dans une même phrase.

5 L'équivalence

Associez chaque expression à son équivalent.

a. I smell a rat. •	• Ça coûte les yeux de la tête.
b. Mind the gap. •	• Ils se vendent comme des petits pains.
c. They are selling like hot cakes. •	• Il y a anguille sous roche.
d. It costs the earth. •	• Attention à la marche.

6 L'emploi des déterminants

Complétez les phrases suivantes avec les déterminants qui conviennent.

a. A good white farmer promised freedom to his slave.

→ Un bon fermier blanc promit .... liberté à son esclave.

b. She's cut her finger while preparing dinner.

→ Elle s'est coupé .... doigt alors qu'elle préparait le dîner.

c. When I was a child, I used to dress up as a pirate.

→ Lorsque j'étais .... enfant, je me déguisais en .... pirate.

7 La voix passive et la voix active

She was engrossed in English literature. She was said to be a bookworm and was learned indeed. Yet, the Romantics eluded her until she was offered Wordsworth's *Lyrical Ballads*. She quickly read them all and was thus turned into a Romantic herself.

1. Avec deux couleurs différentes, soulignez les différents types de verbes :

verbes à la voix passive	verbes à la voix active

2. Traduisez le texte en choisissant la voix qui convient.

OBJECTIF BAC

8 Traduction en français (1)

LE SUJET

Traduisez cet extrait tiré de l'article de Karen McVeigh, « Exiled Chagos Islanders Dream of Return », publié dans *The Guardian* en juin 2019.

The Chagos Islanders have had few victories in their long battle to return from British-enforced exile to their archipelago homeland in the Indian Ocean.

But small steps keep their campaign alive and it is hoped a documentary that will premiere on Saturday will exert pressure on the UK government to change its stance.

Britain's ongoing occupation of the islands was declared illegal in February in an "advisory opinion" by the international court of justice at The Hague. Last month, the UN general assembly showed overwhelming support for a motion setting a six-month deadline for a withdrawal from the Chagos Islands so the archipelago could be reunified with Mauritius.

CONSEILS

- *Chagos Islanders* = Chagossiens
- Utilisez la modulation pour traduire *keep their campaign alive* par « les encouragent à poursuivre la lutte ».

9 Traduction en français (2)

Traduisez cet extrait tiré de *Angela's Ashes, a Memoir of Childhood* (1996), de Frank McCourt.

My father and mother should have stayed in New York where they met and married and where I was born. Instead, they returned to Ireland when I was four, my brother, Malachy, three, the twins, Oliver and Eugene, barely one, and my sister, Margaret, dead and gone.

When I look back on my childhood I wonder how I survived at all. It was, of course, a miserable childhood: the happy childhood is hardly worth your while. Worse than the ordinary miserable childhood is the miserable Irish childhood, and worse yet is the miserable Irish Catholic childhood.

People everywhere brag and whimper about the woes of their early years, but nothing can compare with the Irish version.

Frank McCourt, *Angela's Ashes, a Memoir of Childhood* (1996) © HarperCollins UK.

CORRIGÉS

SE TESTER QUIZ

1 Traduire le lexique

1. a. annoyed: informal / colloquial • b. pissed off: vulgar / slang • c. discontented: formal

2. a. bestioles inoubliables • b. admirer des peintures rupestres • c. des dossiers impossibles à obtenir

2 Utiliser les procédés de traduction

1. Réponses a et d. • L'affirmation b est fausse. La transposition induit un changement de catégorie grammaticale. • L'affirmation c est fausse. C'est possible à l'aide de l'équivalence.

3 Résoudre les problèmes de traduction

1. Réponse b. *'s* après chaque prénom, donc ils ne sont pas frère et sœur. *Talk sb into* + V-*ing* = *convince sb to* + BV.

2. Réponse a. L'imparfait est induit par *and all the while* (= activité régulière).

3. Réponse b. Le *past perfect* n'a pas la même valeur dans les deux occurrences (situation qui perdure / élément déclencheur antérieur).

S'ENTRAÎNER

4 La transposition et la modulation

a. Il finit par entrer en titubant dans le canot de sauvetage. (transpositions et modulation métonymique) • b. Ses ongles sont très négligés. (modulation assertive) • c. Une certaine Mme Jones n'arrête pas de téléphoner (étoffement et modulation assertive) • d. Pense à prendre / ramener les enfants ! (modulation assertive)

5 L'équivalence

a. I smell a rat. Il y a anguille sous roche. • b. Mind the gap. Attention à la marche. • c. They are selling like hot cakes. Ils se vendent comme des petits pains. • d. It costs the earth. Ça coûte les yeux de la tête.

6 L'emploi des déterminants

a. Un bon fermier blanc promit la liberté à son esclave. • b. Elle s'est coupé le doigt alors qu'elle préparait le dîner. • c. Lorsque j'étais Ø enfant, je me déguisais en Ø pirate.

7 La voix passive et la voix active

1. Verbes à la voix active : was, cared for, was learned, eluded.
Verbes à la voix passive : was said to be, was offered, was turned into.

2. Elle était passionnée par la littérature anglaise. On disait d'elle qu'elle était un rat de bibliothèque et elle était très savante. Seulement, la poésie romantique lui échappait jusqu'à ce que les *Ballades Lyriques* de Wordsworth lui furent offertes / qu'on lui offrit / offre les *B. L.* de Wordsworth. Elle les lut toutes rapidement et en fut ainsi changée en **romantique**.

CONSEIL
En français, les **adjectifs substantivés** qui se rapportent aux mouvements littéraires n'ont jamais de majuscule : les romantiques, les humanistes.

OBJECTIF BAC

8 Traduction en français (1)

Les Chagossiens ont connu peu de victoires dans leur long combat pour mettre fin à l'exil imposé par les Britanniques et rentrer chez eux dans leur archipel de l'océan Indien [modulation et étoffement].
Mais de petits progrès les encouragent à poursuivre la lutte et on espère qu'un documentaire qui va sortir / sortira samedi fera pression sur le gouvernement britannique / du Royaume-Uni pour qu'il change de position / modifie sa politique.
L'occupation britannique persistante des îles a été déclarée illégale par la Cour internationale de justice de La Haye dans un « avis consultatif » en février [modification de l'ordre des compléments]. Le mois dernier, l'assemblée générale des Nations Unies a largement adopté une motion fixant un délai de six mois pour évacuer les îles Chagos et ainsi les réunifier à la République mauricienne [choix de verbes pour éviter la répétition et la lourdeur d'une succession de noms].

9 Traduction en français (2)

Mon père et ma mère auraient dû / auraient mieux fait de rester à New York où ils s'étaient rencontrés et mariés et où j'étais né [concordance des temps]. Au lieu de cela, ils étaient retournés / rentrés en Irlande quand j'avais quatre ans, mon frère Malachy, trois ans, les jumeaux Oliver et Eugene, à peine un an, et ma sœur Margaret était morte et enterrée.
Quand je repense à mon enfance je me demande comment j'ai survécu tout simplement / Quand je revois mon enfance, le seul fait d'avoir survécu m'étonne. Ce fut bien sûr une enfance malheureuse [choisir la collocation plutôt que la traduction littérale par *misérable*] : l'enfance heureuse vaut rarement qu'on s'y arrête / s'y intéresse. Pire que l'enfance malheureuse banale / ordinaire, il y a [modulation] l'enfance malheureuse d'Irlandais [transposition]. Et pire encore, il y a l'enfance malheureuse de catholiques irlandais [transposition suivie].
Partout [déplacement en début de phrase pour rendre compte de la place inhabituelle de *everywhere*] les gens se vantent et se plaignent des malheurs de leurs jeunes [modulation] années mais rien ne vaut la variante irlandaise.

7 Réussir l'épreuve orale

L'épreuve orale n'est pas une gageure : le dossier et le propos s'élaborent au fur et à mesure et l'aisance se construit au fil des entraînements.

34 Construire le dossier

En bref *À l'issue de deux années d'enseignement de la spécialité LLCE vous serez évalué à l'écrit comme à l'oral. La partie orale s'appuie sur un dossier personnel que vous présenterez en anglais et dont la préparation requiert réflexion et minutie.*

I Composer le dossier

1 Personnaliser le dossier

- Vous devez constituer votre dossier (*set of documents*) de manière autonome, autour d'une **problématique** (*key question*).
- Pour ce faire, vous pouvez vous servir de documents étudiés en classe et ajouter des documents personnels trouvés lors de vos lectures et différentes recherches ou de vos sorties. Ce dossier est composé de 6 à 8 documents textuels et /ou iconographiques dont le fil conducteur se rattache à une ou plusieurs thématiques du programme du cycle terminal, c'est-à-dire « Rencontre », « Imaginaire », « Arts et débats d'idées », « Expression et construction de soi » ou « Voyages, territoires, frontières ».

INFO
La **problématique** est la question posée en début de **présentation**, à laquelle vous devez répondre grâce à la mise en relation de vos différents documents.

2 Varier la nature des documents

Le dossier doit comprendre…

- au moins **1 texte non littéraire** (article de presse, extrait de discours, d'essai, etc.). → FICHE 22
- au moins **1 des œuvres intégrales** littéraires ou filmiques étudiées en cours (matérialisée par un extrait ou une illustration). → ANNEXES
- au maximum **2 œuvres d'art visuel** (affiche, caricature, dessin, extrait de film, peinture, sculpture, etc.). → FICHE 23
- au moins **2 textes littéraires**, sans se limiter au genre romanesque ; vous pouvez prendre appui sur les annexes publiées avec les programmes, mais aussi, si vous le jugez pertinent, enrichir votre dossier de textes littéraires de votre choix. → FICHE 19

II Assembler le dossier

1 Choisir les documents

- Sélectionnez des documents qui illustrent la ou les thématique·s choisie·s et apportent des éléments **complémentaires et / ou contradictoires** pour répondre à votre problématique.
- Ces documents doivent former un ensemble cohérent et riche, permettant de développer une argumentation dynamique qui s'appuie sur des **va-et-vient constants** entre ceux-ci.

2 Ordonner les documents

- L'organisation du dossier et la définition de la problématique sont intimement liées. C'est en cherchant en quoi chaque document apporte un éclairage différent sur le·s thème·s du dossier que vous affinerez votre problématique. Celle-ci doit soulever un questionnement portant **sur l'intégralité du dossier** et non sur deux ou trois documents uniquement.
- Les documents peuvent être agencés selon un ordre **chronologique**, **diachronique** ou thématique.

INFO
ordre **chronologique** : du plus ancien au plus récent •
ordre **diachronique** : suivant l'évolution des faits dans le temps

zoOm

Enrichir sa culture générale

Fréquenter régulièrement des sites anglophones vous permet à la fois d'améliorer votre anglais et d'enrichir votre culture générale.

- **Chaînes d'information et journaux :**
  - → BBC news – www.bbc.com/news
  - → ABC news – abcnews.go.com
  - → The Guardian – www.theguardian.com
  - → The New York Times – www.nytimes.com
- **Visites virtuelles de musées :**
  - → Tate Modern – www.tate.org.uk
  - → Guggenheim Museum – www.guggenheim.org
  - → National Museum of African American History and Culture – maahc.si.edu
- **Vidéos éducatives :**
  - → Geography now – bit.ly/PbacAngTle_34a
  - → History – bit.ly/PbacAngTle_34b
  - → Every Frame A Painting.com (cinema) – bit.ly/PbacAngTle_34c

35 Présenter le dossier

En bref *La présentation orale du dossier requiert une préparation minutieuse pour répondre aux exigences de l'exercice et aux critères d'évaluation. Il faut bien comprendre ce que l'on attend de vous pour montrer votre maîtrise des attendus du programme de l'enseignement de spécialité pour le cycle terminal.*

I Comprendre les modalités de l'épreuve

1 Maîtriser le déroulé de l'épreuve

- Il n'y a pas de temps de préparation. Vous donnerez un exemplaire du dossier à l'examinateur au début de votre prestation. Vous avez ensuite **dix minutes pour présenter votre dossier** sans intervention de l'examinateur.
- Cette prise de parole en continu est suivie de **dix minutes d'échange** avec l'examinateur. La note maximale de 20/20 valide un niveau C1.

2 Prendre en compte les critères d'évaluation

Vous êtes évalué·e selon des critères précis dans **quatre domaines de compétence**.

Les 4 compétences évaluées

Richesse de la langue : l'étendue de votre répertoire lexical incluant des expressions idiomatiques, des nuances de formulation et des structures variées et complexes.

Expression orale en continu : votre capacité à présenter le dossier en développant une argumentation complexe et fluide à la fois, tout en vous assurant de sa réception.

Correction de la langue orale : votre capacité à vous exprimer dans une langue correcte et fluide, avec une assez bonne maîtrise phonologique.

Interaction orale : votre capacité à participer et construire l'échange tout en exploitant vos connaissances (inter)culturelles.

CONSEIL

Correction et richesse de la langue sont évaluées lors de la prise de parole en continu et de l'interaction, ne l'oubliez pas.

II Réussir la présentation orale

1 Respecter le temps imparti

- Vu le temps court dont vous disposez, il faut être synthétique. Donnez vos arguments et illustrez-les en faisant référence aux documents avec précision. Cela justifiera la constitution de votre dossier. L'introduction et la conclusion doivent respecter un timing strict : pas plus de deux minutes chacune.
- Vos références aux documents doivent être faites avec exactitude pour permettre à l'examinateur de vous suivre facilement.
- Pour favoriser la réception de votre présentation, il faut adopter une méthode claire et s'y conformer. Ainsi, avancer un argument et l'illustrer systématiquement par un exemple rend votre discours plus efficace.

2 Structurer la présentation

- Dans l'introduction, précisez la ou les thématique·s du dossier, présentez brièvement les **documents**, annoncez la problématique puis donnez le plan en une phrase maximum. Il s'agit de mettre en avant la logique interne du dossier.

CONSEIL
Pour respecter le timing sans précipitation, il vaut mieux donner peu d'information sur les **documents** et privilégier les trois autres points.

- Vous ne pourrez développer que trois points maximum, soulignant les échos entre les documents. Pour que l'on suive bien votre propos, il est primordial de marquer les différentes étapes (*To begin with / Firstly, Secondly, Thirdly…*).
- La conclusion doit être annoncée (*To conclude…*) et répondre à la problématique. Elle montre que les documents illustrent la thématique. Vous pouvez finir en inscrivant votre dossier dans l'actualité si cela s'y prête.

zoOm

Interpréter les questions lors de l'échange

Comprendre les questions permet d'y apporter des réponses adéquates.

Exemples de questions	Ce que l'on attend
Could you be specific about…? You mentioned… but it's slightly confusing; could you explain?	Préciser
What devices are used to show that…? Could you develop…?	Approfondir
Can you give instances of / another example of…? What elements show that…?	Illustrer
Don't you think that…? Can you qualify what you said about…?	Reconsidérer un choix

36 Améliorer sa prestation orale

En bref *Sans temps de préparation le jour J, l'épreuve orale suppose un entraînement rigoureux et régulier en amont. Vous devez faire une prestation fluide et maîtriser la phonologie anglaise.*

I S'entraîner à l'épreuve

1 Préparer la prise de parole

■ Les dix premières minutes de votre présentation évalueront votre aptitude à vous exprimer de manière fluide, toute tentative d'apprendre par cœur et de réciter est à proscrire. Pour ce faire, vous devez vous entraîner régulièrement à prendre la parole à partir de vos notes afin de gagner en aisance.

■ Pour parler à partir de notes, celles-ci doivent être visuelles et élaborées avec soin. Elles doivent reproduire votre plan à l'aide de mots-clés, de schémas, de chiffres, de dates et d'exemples. Ne rédigez pas vos phrases en intégralité. Vous pouvez ajouter des connecteurs logiques → FICHE 27 ou des **gap fillers** comme :

Actually... Er... Well you see... Well, what I'm trying to say / to get at is... So my point is... Let me think... Anyway...

> **VOCABULARY**
> **gap fillers** : mots ou expressions qui permettent de gagner du temps pour réfléchir lors d'une prise de parole

2 Répéter dans les conditions réelles

■ Lors de vos phases d'entraînement, il faut répéter votre discours à haute voix à l'aide de vos notes, et pourquoi pas vous filmer. En visionnant votre prestation vous pourrez vérifier si vous parvenez à adopter un ton naturel, une expression fluide, une posture et un temps de parole convenables.

■ Faites une courte pause entre vos différentes parties, adoptez le bon rythme : ni trop rapide, ni trop lent, pour rester convaincant·e et éviter de faire une présentation monotone.

II Améliorer sa prononciation

> **INFO**
> Dans les transcriptions phonétiques, l'accent de mot est matérialisé par un petit trait vertical placé devant la **syllabe accentuée** : ˈ.

1 Bien prononcer et accentuer chaque mot

■ Pour vérifier la prononciation d'un mot, il faut consulter sa transcription phonétique → RABATS dans un dictionnaire ou utiliser les sites qui permettent de l'écouter (wordreference.com, linguee.com). Il convient aussi de respecter l'accent de mot. Les mots anglais de deux syllabes ou plus ont toujours une **syllabe accentuée** : *dramatic* [drəˈmætɪk].

■ Familiarisez-vous avec les règles de base.

• La plupart des noms ou adjectifs de **deux syllabes** sont accentués sur la première syllabe, alors que les verbes de deux syllabes sont accentués sur la seconde syllabe :

comfort (n), **aw**ful (adj), **coun**try (n) – re**turn** (v), de**pend** (v), e**ject** (v)

• Les mots terminés par *-ic, -tion, -sion, -cian* sont accentués sur l'avant-dernière syllabe :

infor**ma**tion, dis**cus**sion, mu**si**cian, re**vi**sion, eco**no**mic

• Mais on compte aussi des **irrégularités** comme :

ho**tel**, ex**am**, **hap**pen, **fi**nish

2 Respecter l'accent de phrase

■ Vous devez respecter la **musicalité de la langue** pour produire des énoncés le plus authentique possible : intonation descendante dans les phrases déclaratives, montante dans les questions fermées (*yes-no questions*) et les énumérations.

■ De plus, la succession des accents de mots donne le rythme de la phrase. L'accentuation étant une **question de contrastes**, certains mots sont prononcés de manière plus marquée que d'autres (*stressed and unstressed words*).

■ Généralement les **mots porteurs de sens** sont accentués : noms, verbes, adjectifs qualificatifs, adverbes, mots interrogatifs, auxiliaires avec négation. Alors que les **mots grammaticaux** (articles, conjonctions, auxiliaires sans négation, déterminants possessifs, relatifs…) ne le sont pas.

zoOm

Gérer ses émotions

Un entraînement régulier permet d'aborder l'épreuve serein·e et confiant·e. Mais la prise de parole suscite souvent une forme d'appréhension.

Comment gérer son stress ?

Se préparer mentalement
L'épreuve n'est plus un saut dans l'inconnu. Visualisez le déroulé de votre prestation orale afin d'anticiper réactions et questions.

Rester positif
Débarrassez-vous des pensées négatives : non, vous n'avez pas « tout oublié ». Souriez, le stress, raisonnable, est une énergie positive et développera votre confiance.

Éliminer les effets du stress
Respirez lentement et profondément pour libérer les tensions. N'allez pas trop vite, parlez clairement et suffisamment fort.

37 Être à l'aise à l'oral

En bref *Le fond de votre prestation doit prévaloir, mais vous devez également maîtriser votre voix, votre gestuelle et être capable de réagir avec à-propos.*

I Maîtriser la communication non verbale

1 Contrôler la gestuelle

- Votre message est véhiculé par votre corps tout entier. Évitez les gestes de fermeture comme par exemple les bras croisés. Adoptez une posture ouverte et stable : grandissez-vous.
- Adoptez une gestuelle naturelle. Que vous ayez tendance à parler avec les mains ou pas, il est important de rester fidèle à votre style personnel, mais restez sobre.

2 Contrôler le regard

- La communication passe aussi par le regard. Établissez tout de suite le contact visuel avec l'examinateur en le regardant dans les yeux. Ne fuyez pas son regard, même si vous êtes intimidé·e.
- Tout au long de votre prestation, vous devez maintenir ce contact avec l'examinateur. Mais sans le fixer de manière exagérée. Votre attitude ne doit pas créer une gêne ou une impression de défiance.

II Interagir avec l'examinateur

1 Entretenir un échange fluide

- Une fois votre présentation terminée, la phase d'interaction avec l'examinateur commence. Vous devez être à même de réagir rapidement et de manière adéquate en utilisant des expressions vous permettant de maintenir et faire progresser l'interaction avec l'examinateur.
- Si vous réalisez que l'examinateur perd le fil, n'hésitez pas à reformuler ou expliquer votre idée à l'aide d'exemples. À l'inverse, en cas d'incompréhension d'une question, soyez prêt·e à utiliser des expressions telles que :

  Would you mind repeating, please? Are you saying that...? What do you mean by...?

2 Savoir argumenter

- De manière générale, quelles que soient les idées exprimées, soyez convaincant·e et justifiez toujours vos propos. Mémorisez quelques structures permettant de rebondir sur un argument et d'exprimer l'accord ou le désaccord.

Structures pour...

Reformuler
Actually... As a matter of fact... What I'm trying to get at is that...

Exprimer votre point de vue personnel
To me... To my mind... It seems to me that... I believe that... I have the feeling that...

Rebondir sur un argument
Yes, I suppose so. However... Well, in a way, but... That may be true but...

Exprimer votre accord ou désaccord
Absolutely true! ... I totally agree with you... That's exactly what I think... I completely disagree with you... I really can't agree ...

■ Le **ton employé** rendra aussi votre propos convaincant, il faut parler d'une **voix claire et posée.** Respectez l'intonation des phrases, une voix monocorde devient vite ennuyeuse.

zoOm

Que faire de vos mains pendant que vous parlez ?

Évitez les gestes parasites qui risquent de détourner l'attention de l'examinateur.

✗ Jouer avec ses bijoux

✗ Se gratter ou tirer sur sa manche

✗ Jouer avec son stylo

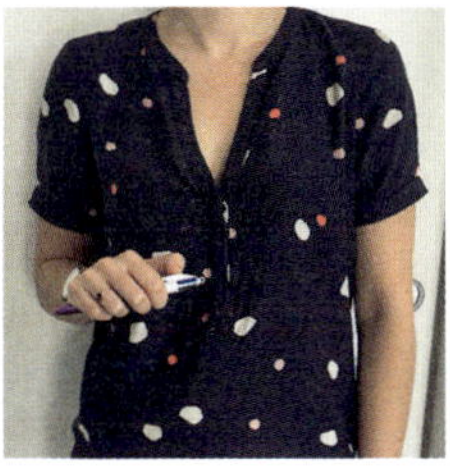

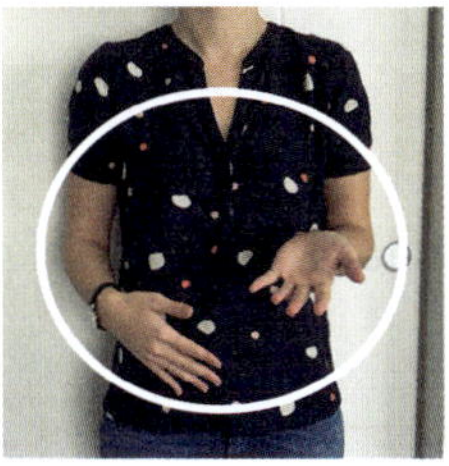

✔ Imaginer un cercle de cette taille et garder toujours ses mains à l'intérieur.

MÉMO VISUEL

Choisissez une ou plusieurs thématiques du cycle terminal

- Prenez une thématique **qui vous parle**.
- Faites-en le **fil conducteur** de votre dossier.

Sélectionnez 6 à 8 documents variés et complémentaires

- Variez les **types de documents** en respectant les consignes.
- Choisissez des documents qui se **complètent** et se **répondent**.

1 Construire le dossier

Construisez votre dossier personnel

- Définissez une problématique qui prend en compte l'**intégralité** des documents.
- **Ordonnez** les documents de façon cohérente.

Réussi

4 Améliorer son expression orale

Gagnez en fluidité

- Entraînez-vous à parler **à partir de notes** élaborées minutieusement.
- Multipliez vos phases d'**entrainement** et filmez-vous.

Gagnez en authenticité

- Prêtez attention à votre **débit** de parole.
- Concentrez-vous sur l'**intonation** et la **prononciation**.
- Ne négligez pas la **syntaxe**.

'épreuve orale

2 Présenter le dossier

Justifiez le choix des documents
- Montrez qu'ils **répondent** à votre problématique.
- Montrez en quoi ils **illustrent** la ou les thématiques.

Respectez le temps imparti
- Présentez une **argumentation** complexe et synthétique.
- Formulez une **introduction** succincte et consacrez davantage de temps aux arguments.
- Ménagez des **transitions** claires.

3 Être à l'aise à l'oral

Favorisez la communication
- Adoptez une **posture** ouverte et stable.
- Évitez toute **attitude** de repli sur soi (bras croisés, épaules courbées…).
- Gérez le **stress**.

Interagissez efficacement
- Efforcez-vous de comprendre ce que les **questions** impliquent.
- Utilisez des **expressions clés**.
- N'hésitez pas à **reformuler** votre propos.

Maintenez l'attention du correcteur
- Accrochez le **regard** de l'interlocuteur.
- Soyez **convaincant·e**.
- Parlez d'une **voix** claire et posée.

SE TESTER QUIZ

Vérifiez que vous avez bien compris les points clés des **fiches 34 à 37**.

1 Construire et présenter le dossier

→ FICHES 34 ET 35

1. Complétez le texte ci-dessous avec les mots qui conviennent.

Pour construire mon dossier, je choisis une .... qui me plaît et qui sera mon fil conducteur. Je peux sélectionner .... à .... documents .... et .... Je dois définir une .... qui prend en compte .... des documents et les .... de façon cohérente.

2. Vrai ou faux ? Cochez la case qui convient.

	V	F
a. Le jour de l'épreuve, j'aurai 10 mn de préparation.	☐	☐
b. Ma présentation se compose de deux parties de 15 mn.	☐	☐
c. Il est conseillé d'annoncer un plan détaillé dans l'introduction.	☐	☐
d. Il est conseillé de développer trois points au maximum.	☐	☐

2 Améliorer sa présentation orale

→ FICHE 36

1. Cochez les réponses correctes.

Vous devez vous appuyer sur des notes claires comportant :

☐ a. des chiffres et des dates
☐ b. une introduction courte
☐ c. des mots-clés
☐ d. des exemples

2. Placez l'accent de mot (petit trait vertical) correctement.

expression (n) • horrid (adj) • evoke (vb) • iconic (adj) • acculturation (n)

3. Associez chaque mot à sa transcription phonétique.

a. ferociousness •	• [ˈθæŋkfʊl]
b. thankful •	• [fəˈɡɪvnɪs]
c. forgiveness •	• [ˈθaʊzənd]
d. thousand •	• [fəˈrəʊʃəsnəs]

3 Être à l'aise à l'oral

→ FICHE 37

Associez les expressions suivantes avec leur fonction.

a. That's exactly what I think! •	• Exprimer l'accord / le désaccord
b. Yes, I suppose so. However... •	• Reformuler
c. What I'm trying to get at is that... •	• Rebondir sur un argument

S'ENTRAÎNER

Le dossier proposé dans les exercices qui suivent porte sur les thématiques « Art et débats d'idées » et « Voyages, territoires, frontières ».

Il permet d'explorer comment l'art s'inscrit dans le débat d'idées, notamment quand des relations communautaires sont marquées par des tensions extrêmes dans un territoire donné. Il soulève les questions suivantes : l'art est-il forcément contestataire dans un pays traumatisé par des années de conflit meurtrier : l'**Irlande du Nord** ? Peut-il jouer un autre rôle ?

HELP
Watch a short history of Northern Ireland:
bit.ly/PbacAngTle_Ireland

4 Exploiter un film comme œuvre complète

Utilisez l'analyse du film → ANNEXES 3 ET 4 **pour répondre aux questions.**

Document A

This 2002 multi-award-winning film by Paul Greengrass explores one particular event of the Troubles known as Bloody Sunday

1. Say if these statements are right or wrong.

	R	W
a. This film is a documentary fiction.	☐	☐
b. The soundtrack is not prioritised to highlight chaos.	☐	☐
c. Parallel editing shows the two opposite sides at once.	☐	☐
d. Various characters seem to be inert, hindered by circumstances.	☐	☐

2. Fill in the blanks.

Thanks to his direction, Paul G............. clearly blames the British s............. for the m............. but without spreading propaganda and by carefully examining the shared r............. of both s............. We understand the director's political m............. at the end of the film when Bernadette Devlin proclaims: "We will not rest until justice is done."

5 Exploiter un extrait de fiction

Lisez l'extrait et répondez aux questions.

Document B

A mother has moved from Derry to a caravan in Galway with her thirteen-year-old son Kevin. The boy regularly gets news from his uncle who is an IRA prisoner and has started a hunger strike.

It was the twenty-first day and she told him his uncle had lost seventy pounds and that the food was still kept at the bottom of the bed like an equinox between life and death. He was still in the cell block, but might soon be removed to the prison hospital. It was said that his spirits were good, although his cough was tearing at his chest and he found it hard to swallow water. He was reading books for the first time in years, poetry and a play by W.B. Yeats. When he opened the Perspex window of his cell he could hear the Orangemen outside the prison gates, playing their lambeg drums[1], and it was like slow torture to him.

She gave the boy a newspaper and he was surprised to remember that other people had lives too. An elderly woman had been killed by a soldier who had thought that the umbrella she carried was a rifle. A young father was shot coming out of a maternity ward. A tightrope walker from France had been set on fire as he tried to walk a rope between two housing estates in Derry – a Molotov cocktail had hit against his knee and he had continued walking as the flames rose high around him, dropping finally into the Foyle, his balance pole lost in the dark waters below him. On the streets the rioting was worse than before, burning barricades, tear gas, rubber bullets, checkpoints.

There was still no news of a breakthrough, although some international committees were involved now too, everyone was clamouring for a solution, it had to come soon, it was inevitable. (...)

How long was the longest hunger strike? He asked.

Sixty-something days.

And the shortest?

Oh please, Kevin, let's not talk anymore about it.

It was forty days or so, wasn't it?

Just go to bed. Please, son. Please.

I'm just asking you.

And I'm just asking you, go on to bed, please.

He couldn't sleep, rose from his bed at four, tiptoed across the caravan, stole eighteen pounds from his mother's handbag and went down to the town. (...) He fired stones at each of the three traffic lights in town and smashed the amber glass of one, found himself sprinting with imaginary policemen following. (...)

He found himself walking along the coast road until he managed to hitch a lift in a farmer's pick-up truck. (...) He was dropped off in the city centre.

Thanks, he said to the farmer and under his breath he muttered: Ye humpy cunt.

The city was in full throat. (...) On telegraph poles there hung signs that said: *Support the Hunger Strikers!* And from a balcony on Dominik Street black flags fluttered. The boy punched his fist in the air. (...)

At the bus station he bought a ticket and played video games until he heard the announcement over the tannoy[2]. He boarded with a swagger[3]. (...)

When the bus driver mentioned over the microphone about a connection to Derry City from Donegal town the boy punched his fist in the air once more and said: Brits Out, Me In.

Colum McCann, "Hunger Strike", a novella published in *Everything in this Country Must* (2000).

1. lambeg drums: large Irish drums primarily used by unionists
2. tannoy: loudspeaker
3. swagger: self-important walk (*en se pavanant*)

1. Say if these statements are right or wrong.

	R	W
a. Kevin's uncle will be a political prisoner after his hunger strike.	☐	☐
b. Kevin's grasp of the conflict is limited and based on hearsay.	☐	☐
c. Kevin is obsessed by his uncle's hunger strike which he considers as a Christ-like sacrifice.	☐	☐
d. The violence of the conflict is all the more unacceptable as it kills innocent people in horrendous ways.	☐	☐
e. People in Galway don't feel concerned by the conflict at all.	☐	☐

2. Use different colours to highlight the elements referring to:

- violence
- the inability to relate (with the living)
- impossible reconciliation.

3. Complete this sentence with the right propositions to draw your conclusion. The parallel which can be drawn between the Troubles in Northern Ireland and Kevin's life in Galway shows that...

☐ **a.** ... the Troubles pervade Kevin's life and trigger his behavior.
☐ **b.** ... Kevin is lightly affected by the conflict in Northern Ireland.
☐ **c.** ... it is impossible to escape the trauma induced by the conflict in Northern Ireland.
☐ **d.** ... the conflict is fuelled by hatred which is passed on to younger generations.

4. Find an example of **paratactic style** and an unusual association suggesting irony in the extract. What idea do they subtly convey?

VOCABULARY
paratactic style: absence of logical connectors and even speech markers

5. Use these words to fill in the blanks: *ironically, paratactic, pointless, subtle, unacceptable.*

Colum McCann's .... style and his .... suggesting that "having lives" means dying .... denounce violence and destruction as both .... and ....

6 Exploiter des fresques murales

Étudiez ces deux fresques murales et répondez aux questions.

Documents C et D

The first mural (C) is one of the 12 murals commemorating the Battle of the Bogside and Bloody Sunday. The second mural (D) was painted over a sectarian mural, as part of the Reimaging Communities programme. The former mural showed the emblem of the Ulster Defense Association, a Unionist paramilitary group.

1. Focus on the mural C. Choose the correct answers.

a. The gas-mask represents a way to:

☐ protect oneself from danger and challenge the police.

☐ remain anonymous and become representative of all children from the Bogside.

☐ stress the destitution of the population from the Bogside.

b. Portraying a child is a way to:

☐ initiate emotional reactions from viewers.

☐ depict a helpless victim of his environment.

☐ highlight vulnerability and innocence have gone.

c. The goal of the mural is to:

☐ offer an olive branch to nationalists.

☐ denounce police violence and chronicle a crucial moment in the recent History of the Bogside.

☐ make sure nobody will ever forget people's sufferings.

2. Focus on the mural D. Match each element from the left to a colour and its symbolism as in the example.

Element from the mural	Corresponding colour	Symbolism
• a lonely girl • barbed wire, paramilitaries, soldier • a globe • a dove • groups of children	• blue and green • grey • lively colours • white • grey	• stand for terrorism • promote peace • express sadness and grief • promote cohesion • promote multiculturalism

3. Deduce the main messages of the mural, choose the correct answers.

☐ **a.** The mural is meant to express hope for the future, thanks to younger generations.
☐ **b.** The mural is meant to pay tribute to victims terrorism.
☐ **c.** The mural is meant to advocate peace and the end of armed conflicts.

4. Complete this sentence to compare the murals.

The petrol bomber on the mural on the left epitomizes .... while the dove on the mural on the right sends .... for the future.

7 Exploiter un article de presse

Lisez le texte et répondez aux questions.

Document E

This article discusses the pros and cons of the murals and their touristic impact.

'Troubles tourism': should Derry be celebrating its political murals?

Fifty years since the Battle of the Bogside, some fear the new status of Derry's murals as a tourist attraction will stop the community overcoming the past.

One of the first things you see as you enter Bogside is a 20ft mural of a 12-year-old boy, wearing a gas mask and clutching a petrol bomb.

Painted on the side of a social housing property, it's a stark reminder of the violence that tore Derry apart during the Troubles. One of a series of 12 murals telling the story of Bloody Sunday. (...)

This week marks 50 years since the battle, and Tom Kelly, one of the Bogside artists who painted the mural in the early 1990s, says his image shows "a community standing up for basic civil and human rights". It is not intended to be partisan, he says. "I don't see it as violent or sinister."

When it first went up, however, Kelly says it was heavily criticised in both the Times and the Irish Times for glorifying pre-teen violence. The Bogside murals have remained divisive ever since, not just among Protestants but among local Catholics and republicans who want to shake off the legacy of the past.

They have now also become something else: a tourist attraction. A recent NI Tourism report puts political murals as the eighth most visited attraction in the entire country. The neighbouring Museum of Free Derry, which tells the story of Bloody Sunday, attracted 35,000 visitors in 2018.

According to the tourist board, all coach tours to the city now stop at the murals.

Earlier this year, the local council doubled down. It took a controversial step: it would encourage this so-called "Troubles tourism" by providing funding to illuminate the murals at night. (...)

Some critics say illuminating the murals simply keeps old wounds open. (...)

Indeed, the Troubles are far from consigned to the past. The killing in April of the journalist Lyra McKee in the nearby Creggan neighbourhood, where she was observing police raids on republican dissidents, was a reminder that Derry hasn't completely eradicated violence.

New murals, meanwhile, are popping up all the time. (...)

Troubles tourism isn't new in Northern Ireland. It first took off in the early 2000s, says Dominic Bryan, a lecturer at Queen's University Belfast. "People realised that with peace, tourism was on the agenda," he says. "The history is literally painted on the wall, in the memorials. The story of republicanism and loyalism as a narrative is being told all around you. It's very visual: it's fantastic to do a tour."

Unlike murals painted by the IRA or paramilitary groups, the Bogside murals are not affiliated to any political group. Nevertheless, they have been politicised by becoming a "focal point for protest", says Sara McDowell, a lecturer at Ulster University.

"These murals are not passive, they don't just exist there, they're active spaces," she says. "Do they serve to educate people about the past, or do they transfer this sense of trauma and this specific narrative on to new generations?" (...)

Rachel Hall, "'Troubles tourism': should Derry be celebrating its political murals?", *The Guardian*, August 12th, 2019.

1. Complete this chart with quotes from the article to illustrate the controversy over the murals in Belfast.

	Positive effect	Negative effect
The murals	• are an unbiased representation: .... • are a way to educate about the past:	• promote division and hatred: .... • prevent reconciliation: ....
Trouble tourism	• is a popular tourist attraction worth developing for the local council: .... • shows the Troubles are over:	• sends an offensive message: ....

2. Pick up the event which proves that it is hard to "shake off the legacy of the past" and that peace is fragile.

8 Exploiter une chanson

Écoutez et lisez la chanson puis répondez aux questions.

Document F

This medley by the Pogues was so controversial when it was released in 1988 that it was banned from broadcast by the Independent Broadcasting Authority because it alleged that "convicted terrorists were not guilty, the Irish people were put at a disadvantage in the Courts of the UK and that it may have initiated support for a terrorist organization such as the IRA."

À NOTER
Écoutez la chanson : bit.ly/PbacAngTle_Pogues

Streets of Sorrow / Birmingham Six
Oh farewell you streets of sorrow
And farewell you streets of pain
I'll not return to feel more sorrow
Nor to see more young men slain
Through the last six years I've lived through terror
And in the darkened streets the pain
Oh how I long to find some solace
In my mind I curse the strain
So farewell you streets of sorrow
And farewell you streets of pain
No I'll not return to feel more sorrow
Nor to see more young men slain
There were six men in Birmingham, in Guildford there's four[1]
That were picked up and tortured and framed by the law
And the filth got promotion but they're still doing time
For being Irish in the wrong place and at the wrong time
In Ireland they'll put you away in the Maze[2]
In England they'll keep you for seven long days
God help you if ever you're caught on these shores
The coppers need someone And they walk through that door
You'll be counting years– first five, then ten
Growing old in a lonely hell
Round the yard and the stinking cell
From wall to wall, and back again
A curse on the judges, the coppers and screws
Who tortured the innocent, wrongly accused
For the price of promotion and justice to sell
May the judged be their judges when they rot down in hell
You'll be counting years – first five, then ten
Growing old in a lonely hell
Round the yard and the lousy cell
From wall to wall, and back again
May the whores of the empire lie awake in their beds
And sweat as they count out the sins on their heads

While over in Ireland eight more men lie dead
Kicked down and shot in the back of the head[3]
You'll be counting years
First five, then ten
Growing old in a freezing hell
Round the yard and the lousy cell
From wall to wall, and back again
Counting years
First five, then ten
Growing old in a lonely hell
Round the yard and the lousy cell
From wall to wall, and back again

The Pogues, "Streets of Sorrow / Birmingham Six", Compositeur et auteur : Woods Terence.

1. The Birmingham Six and the Guilford Four: Irishmen accused of bombing pubs and killing people in England 1974; they spent 16 and 15 years in prison before the sentence was overturned. They were still in prison when the song was released.
2. The Maze: Long Kesh prison in Belfast where all IRA activists or suspected activists and suspected sympathizers were kept.
3. Allusion to the Loughgall Ambush where IRA activists fell into a trap and were shot dead by British soldiers in may 1987. One civilian was also killed by the soldiers.

1. The song is clearly made of two different parts, what part of the song do these elements correspond to?

	Part 1	Part 2
a. a gentle acoustic ballad with a regular slow rhythm and a melancholy tune and song	☐	☐
b. Celtic punk rock with an aggressive feel, a fast rhythm, a coarse voice	☐	☐
c. a political message targeting the British government, judicial system and anti-Irish sentiment in Britain	☐	☐
d. feelings evolving from anger to wrath and leading to insulting and even cursing those who are held responsible	☐	☐
e. feelings evolving from sorrow to anguish	☐	☐
f. Northern Islanders facing racism and injustice wherever they are	☐	☐
g. exile as the only viable solution to avoid the Troubles	☐	☐
h. protest and rebellion as the means to change an unacceptable and unfair situation	☐	☐
i. emotional lament over the destruction of both territory and people	☐	☐
j. clear accusation based on the mention of particular events	☐	☐

2. Tick the elements which show why these two parts of the song unite into a successful medley.

☐ **a.** exploring the ongoing Troubles
☐ **b.** despondency exploding into rage
☐ **c.** Northern Islanders as victims, whether in NI or in England
☐ **d.** a controversial hard-hitting song exploring a controversial topic
☐ **e.** triggering sympathy and urge people to react and do something about it

☐ **f.** two contradictory visions of the Troubles
☐ **g.** common features: alternate rhymes and repetitions of vocabulary, sounds and even stanzas, together with slight variations
☐ **h.** no similar patterns between the two parts

OBJECTIF BAC

Les documents (A, B, C, D, E et F) que vous venez d'étudier constituent le dossier oral sur lequel vous allez vous appuyer pour faire les exercices suivants.

9 Construire son discours

1. List the documents you could use in these parts of your presentation.

I. Mirroring the conflict: Documents..................
II. Transmitting the legacy of the conflict: Documents..................
III. Discussing reconciliation: Documents..................

2. Complete the outline of your presentation with elements and quotes.

I. Mirroring the conflict

1. Emotional testimony

- Genuine snapshots showing brutal violence and the pain it causes to trigger anguish and sympathy. Document .... : ....
- Careful reconstructions and re-creations showing unacceptable and inevitable chaos to shock and baffle. Document .... : ....

2. Real protest

- Pinpointing unacceptable violence and destruction in a subtle way to denounce unfairness and nonsense. Document .... : ....
- Openly blaming the British government, judicial system and angrily denouncing racism and anti-Irish sentiment to urge people to react and to join contestation. Document ....: ....

[Conclusion] Art as a faithful mirror of the conflict / artistic representations = genuine but partisan, no matter how subtle or obvious denouncing is → controversial (hence some works of art have been banned)

> **CONSEIL**
> Votre **conclusion de partie** doit synthétiser les arguments développés et en dégager l'enjeu central. Reprenez les termes du titre.

II. Transmitting the legacy of the conflict

1. Educating the younger generations

- Giving information about the past and commemorating the victims to make sure no one ever forgets. Document .... : ....
- Representing past events and retelling/rewriting the conflict to grasp the surroundings, family history and the older generations' emotional response to the past. Document .... : ....

2. Maintaining a yawning chasm

- Fuelling hatred by exposing injustice and violence and thus dragging out the conflict. Document .... : ....
- Keeping old wounds open by maintaining suffering alive and thus preventing the fractures from healing: Document .... : ....

[Conclusion] Art as an effective means to transmit the legacy of the conflict but always emotional tinge to it so never neutral therefore = controversial. It also transmits the trauma → it cannot be denied that it contributes to maintaining division

III. Discussing reconciliation

1. Troublesome reconciliation

- Exposing the spiral of violence and hatred to suggest peaceful reconciliation may be difficult. Document .... : ....
- Demanding recognition and compensation to right the ills and wrongs of past policies as a necessary precondition to stop screaming for vengeance. Document .... : ....

2. Laying the foundations of long-term harmony?

- Understanding the mechanism of violence to acknowledge shared responsibilities, to recognize equal sharing of suffering and overcome trauma. Document .... : ....
- Re-imaging the surroundings (= territory) by giving visual art a new role (= tourism) and altering its message to promote inclusion and bridge the gap between communities. Document .... : ....

[Conclusion] Legacy of long lasting conflict and trauma = not that easy to shake off. Steps forward but no real consensus/ bridge the gap = not that obvious + very fragile indeed.

10 Ranger les documents dans le dossier

Now that you have decided on your presentation, choose the most appropriate way to order the documents in your portfolio.

☐ **a.** chronological order ☐ **b.** diachronic order ☐ **c.** thematic order

11 Introduire la présentation

Delete superfluous words, phrases and sentences so as to shorten this introduction and respect a 2mn timing maximum. Make changes if necessary.

[Présentation des documents] There are 6 documents in my portfolio:

❶ *Bloody Sunday* a 2002 multi-award-winning film by Paul Greengrass starring James Nesbitt which dramatizes the traumatic event that turned a peaceful march for civil rights into violence and bloodshed in Derry on Sunday, January 30th, 1972.

❷ An extract from Colum McCann's novella "Hunger Strike" which is part of a collection entitled *Everything in This Country Must*, published in 2000. It focuses on a 13-year-old boy who has moved from Derry to a caravan in Galway and who feels concerned by his uncle's hunger strike.

❸ Two murals which can be seen in Belfast. One mural commemorating the Battle of the Bogside is located in Derry, a Catholic district.

❹ The other one, which was funded by the Re-imaging Communities programme and was painted over a mural promoting the Ulster Defence Association which is a paramilitary group, is located at the corner of Lendrick Street and Newtownards Road, a Unionist district.

❺ An article from Rachel Hall, published in January 2019 in *The Guardian* entitled "'Troubles tourism': should Derry be celebrating its political murals?", which considers the way the murals and Troubles tourism are perceived by people living in Belfast.

❻ A controversial song by Celtic rock band the Pogues entitled "Streets of Sorrow / Birmingham Six" which was released in 1988 and is part of the album "If I Should Fall from Grace". It both laments over the havoc caused by the Troubles and violently accuses the British government of injustice and racism towards Northern Irelanders.

[Problématique] The set of documents illustrates two themes. Indeed, not only does it deal with "art and debate" but also with "travels, territories, frontiers". The documents explore different aspects of the Troubles in Northern Ireland and enable to discuss the effects of the violent outbursts or division it triggered both within Northern Ireland and the bordering countries, both on the country itself and the communities involved, as well as at the time and in the long run. They also show how some artists represented the conflict, addressed the issue and contributed to the heated debate over territory both during and after the Troubles.

They raise the following questions: considering the historical social and political background, is art necessarily a means of protest in Northern Ireland? What role can it play after the Troubles?

[Annonce du plan] In order to answer these questions, I will first show it can be used as a means to mirror the conflict. Then, I will see what role it plays in transmitting the legacy of the conflict. Finally, I will consider how artists discuss (possible) reconciliation through their works of art.

12 Conclure la présentation

Reorder these sentences so as to make a relevant conclusion.

...... a. Yet, art addressing the Troubles also points that a wind of change may be blowing over Northern Ireland even if peace and reconciliation may be fragile indeed as wounds are long to heal, especially emotional ones.
...... b. They do show how some artists represented the conflict and contributed to the heated debate over territory both during and after the Troubles.

...... c. Their works presented in my portfolio both mirror the conflict and transmit its legacy, and are thus controversial as they cannot but be considered as means of protest, whether it be subtle or more obvious and even sheer outrage.
...... d. The different documents explore different aspects of the Troubles in Northern Ireland and enable to discuss the effects of the violent outbursts or division it triggered both within Northern Ireland and the bordering countries, both on the country itself and the communities involved, as well as at the time and in the long run.

13 Anticiper les questions de l'examinateur

To prepare interacting with the examiner, browse these websites to pick out relevant information.

a. bit.ly/PbacAngTle_BSa : ....
b. bit.ly/PbacAngTle_BSb : ....
c. bit.ly/PbacAngTle_BSc : ....
d. bit.ly/PbacAngTle_BSd : ....

CORRIGÉS

SE TESTER QUIZ

1 Construire et présenter le dossier

1. Pour construire mon dossier, je choisis une thématique qui me plaît et qui sera mon fil conducteur. Je peux sélectionner 6 à 8 documents variés et complémentaires. Je dois définir une problématique qui prend en compte l'intégralité des documents et les ordonner de façon cohérente.

2. a. Faux : pas de préparation pour cette épreuve. • b. Faux : 2 fois 10 mn. • c. Faux : un plan succinct est préférable pour respecter le timing. • d. Vrai.

2 Améliorer sa présentation orale

1. Il faut cocher a, c et d.

2. ex'pression • 'horrid • e'voke • i'conic • accultu'ration

3. a. [fəˈrəʊʃəsnəs] • b. [ˈθæŋkfʊl] • c. [fəˈgɪvnɪs] • d. [ˈθaʊzənd]

3 Être à l'aise à l'oral

a. Exprimer l'accord / le désaccord • b. Rebondir sur un argument • c. Reformuler

S'ENTRAÎNER

4 Exploiter un film comme œuvre complète

1. a. Wrong: it is built like a TV report / documentary. • b. Wrong: it is a way to create lifelikeness. • c. Right: thanks to cross-cutting and parallel editing. • d. Right: examples of General Mac Lellan, Superintendent Logan, the British soldier inside the army tank, Ivan Cooper at the hospital (end).

2. Thanks to his direction, Paul Greengrass clearly blames the British soldiers for the massacre but without spreading propaganda and by carefully examining the shared responsibilities of both sides. We understand the director's political message at the end of the film when Bernadette Devlin proclaims: "We will not rest until justice is done."

5 Exploiter un extrait de fiction

1. a. Wrong: (l. 3, 5-6) • b. Right: (l. 1, 4, 10) • c. Right: (l. 22-29) • d. Right: (l. 11-17 à) • e. Wrong: (l. 39-40)

2. violence: "on the streets the rioting was worse than before, burning barricades, tear gas, rubber bullets, checkpoints" (l. 17-18) / "he fired stones at each of the three traffic lights in town and smashed the glass amber of one" (l. 32-33) + "under his breath he muttered: Ye humpy cunt" (l. 37-38)
inability to relate: "He was reading books for the first time in years"(l. 6) / Kevin's mother doesn't answer his questions and says "go to bed" (l. 27)
impossible reconciliation: "he could hear the Orangemen (...) and it was like slow torture to him" (l. 7-9) / "Brits Out, Me In." (l. 46)

3. Il faut cocher : a, c, d.

4. Paratactic style: paragraph 2 • Unusual association suggesting irony: "people had lives" and three people's violent deaths (l. 11)

5. Colum McCann's paratactic style and his ironically suggesting that "having lives" means dying subtly denounce violence and destruction as both unacceptable and pointless.

6 Exploiter des fresques murales

1. a. The gas-mask represents a way to protect oneself, challenge the police, remain anonymous and become representative of all children from the Bogside.
b. Portraying a child is a way to initiate emotional reactions from viewers and highlight vulnerability and innocence have gone.
c. The goal of the mural is to denounce police violence and chronicle a crucial moment in the recent History of the Bogside and make sure nobody will ever forget people's sufferings.

2. • barbed wire, paramilitaries, soldier / grey / stand for terrorism, violence
• a globe / blue and green / promote multiculturalism
• a dove / white / promote peace
• groups of children / lively colours / promote cohesion

3. Il faut cocher a et c.

4. The petrol bomber on the mural on the left epitomizes violence while the dove on the mural on the right sends a hopeful message for the future.

7 Exploiter un article de presse

1.

	Positive effect	Negative effect
The murals	• "a community standing up for basic civil and human rights" (l. 12) / "not intended to be partisan" (l. 12-13) • "The history is literally painted on the walls" (l. 38) / "the story of republicanism and loyalism as a narrative is being told around you" (l. 38-39) / "educate people about the past" (l. 46)	• "a stark reminder of the violence that tore Derry apart" (l. 7-8) • "transfer this sense of trauma and this specific narrative on to new generations" (l. 47-48)
Trouble tourism	• "the eighth most visited attraction in the entire country" (l. 20-21) / "providing funding to illuminate the murals at night" (l. 26-27) • "with peace, tourism was on the agenda" (l. 37)	• "keeps old wounds open" (l. 28)

2. Lines 30 to 33: "the Troubles are far from consigned to the past. The killing in April of journalist Lycra McKee in the nearby Creggan neighbourhood where she was observing police raids on republican dissidents, was a reminder that Derry hasn't completely eradicated violence."

8 Exploiter une chanson

1. Part 1: a, b, g, i • Part 2: c, d, e, f, h, j

2. Il faut cocher : a, b, c, d, e, g.

OBJECTIF BAC

9 Construire son discours

1. I. : Docs A, B, C, F • II. : Docs A, B, C, D, E, F • III. : Docs A, B, D, E

2.

I. Mirroring the conflict

1. Emotional testimony

■ Doc. C: a child wearing a gasmask to protect himself

Doc. D: left part: sad lonely girl looking down + grey colours

Doc. F (part 1): part 1: especially l. 2 ("sorrow") and l. 3 ("pain") + l. 5 ("young men slain") and l. 6 ("terror") + melancholy tone / heartbreaking decision to become an exile

■ **Doc. B:** paragraph 2 last sentence and paragraph 1 + paratactic style
Doc. A: non prioritised sounds and shaky images in the 5mn scene of the massacre + captured life effect like a documentary: vague framing, handheld camera shots

2. Real protest

■ **Doc. B:** "people had lives too" associated with the violent deaths of three innocent people + uncle's death = inevitable (use of passive voice + details about his declining health) and pointless as will never get political status

■ **Doc. F (part 2):** angry protest (rhythm, vocabulary, repetitions): people go to prison "for being Irish in the wrong place and at the wrong time" / the police "tortured the innocent, wrongly accused" / chorus about the conditions of imprisonment
Conclusion: the song was banned when it came out

II. Transmitting the legacy of the conflict

1. Educating the younger generations

■ **Doc. C:** is one of the 12 murals by the Bogside artists commemorating the Battle of the Boyne and Bloody Sunday
Doc. E: "a community standing up for basic rights" / "murals to educate people about the past" / "The history is literally painted on the walls"

■ **Doc. B:** second-hand knowledge of the conflict through the papers ("she gave the boys a newspaper") + by his mother after phone-calls ("she told him" / "he was said to be")
Doc. A: long shot on young men queuing up to join the IRA after the shootings + close-ups on their determined and serious faces

2. Maintaining a yawning chasm

■ **Doc. B:** Kevin's obsession with his uncle's hunger strike leads to a breach in his relationship with his mother ("go on to bed") + fuels violence (stoning traffic lights + insulting the farmer) and hatred ("Brits Out. Me In")

■ **Doc. E:** "keeping old wounds open"/ "transmitting this sense of trauma on to younger generations"/ "a stark reminder of the violence that tore Derry apart"

III. Discussing reconciliation

1. Troublesome reconciliation

■ **Doc. B:** Vicious circle = parallel between 3 violent deaths and stoning "three traffic lights and "smashing" one of them + boarding a bus to leave safe Galway to join the IRA
Doc. E: Mural C as "glorifying pre-teen violence"
Doc. F: Exile to flee terror, impossible to live in "sorrowful streets of Belfast"

■ **Doc. A (end):** close-up on Bernadette Devlin saying "we will not rest until justice is done"

2. Laying the foundations of long-term harmony?

■ **Doc. A:** cross-cutting editing + quick fade out → inescapable tragedy/parallel editing à shared responsibility

■ **Doc. E:** the murals as a popular tourist attraction worth developing ("illuminate" them) Trouble Tourism = a positive sign that the Troubles belong to the past ("With peace, tourism was on the agenda")

Doc. D: Reimaging communities programme + more inclusive and hopeful message (children doing things together, bright colours, dove)
Conclusion: a journalist's death so "Derry hasn't completely eradicated violence" (Doc. E)

10 Ranger les documents dans le dossier

c. thematic order, because of the thematic approach of the presentation and reference to almost all documents in each part.

11 Introduire la présentation

There are 6 documents in my portfolio: *Bloody Sunday,* a 2002 film by Peter Greengrass, which dramatizes the traumatic event that took place on Sunday, January 30th, 1972; an extract from Colum McCann's novella "Hunger Strike", published in 2000, which focuses on a 13-year-old boy who has moved from Derry to Galway; two murals which can be seen in Belfast: one mural is located in Derry and the other one in a Unionist district.
There are also a 2019 article from *The Guardian* about 'Troubles tourism' and a 1988 song by Celtic rock band the Pogues entitled "Streets of Sorrow/ Birmingham Six" which both laments over the havoc caused by the Troubles and accuses the British government of injustice and racism towards Northern Irelanders.
The set of documents illustrates two themes. Indeed, not only does it deal with "art and debate" but also with "travels, territories, frontiers". The documents explore different aspects of the Troubles in Northern Ireland and show how some artists addressed the issue.
They raise the following questions: considering the historical social and political background, is art necessarily a means of protest in Northern Ireland? What role can it play after the Troubles?
In order to answer these questions, I will consider art as a means to mirror the conflict, then the role it plays in transmitting the legacy of the conflict and finally how artists discuss (possible) reconciliation through their works of art.

12 Conclure la présentation

d - b - c - a

13 Anticiper les questions de l'examinateur

a. Paul Greengrass: "All come together and relive the events, and in a spirit of reconciliation, move on." Many extras hired for the film took part in the real events.
b. Two other short stories pointing at trauma and difficult reconciliation; in "Everything in this Country Must" the father kills his favourite horse after the British soldiers save it.
c. The twelve murals all commemorate a specific event. The mural was preserved according to the local people's wish during a renovation project.
d. The programme promotes community cohesion, peace and reconciliation and has led to the creation of 32 pieces of public art all over Northern Ireland.

Annexes

38 Analyser une œuvre littéraire intégrale

En bref *L'analyse d'œuvres intégrales fait partie intégrante de la spécialité LLCE : un extrait de l'une d'entre elles devra obligatoirement apparaître dans la partie orale de l'épreuve. Plusieurs lectures associées à des recherches de fond vous permettront d'analyser l'œuvre.*

I Découvrir l'œuvre pour l'analyser

1 La première lecture

- La première lecture est avant tout une expérience de découverte. Lisez sans préjugés, et sans vouloir aller trop vite vers les axes du programme.
- Cette première lecture doit vous permettre de lever les obstacles de compréhension : au crayon à papier, encadrez les passages que vous trouvez difficiles à comprendre, et faites des recherches systématiques de lexique que vous reprendrez ensuite sous forme de fiches.
- À ce stade, si vous ne rencontrez pas de difficultés majeures de compréhension, il vous est possible de commencer à faire des repérages plus serrés : identifiez qui est le narrateur, qui sont les personnages, et faites une frise chronologique des événements importants dans l'intrigue.

CONSEIL
Vous devez faire vos recherches de **lexique** avec un dictionnaire bilingue, pour lever les difficultés de compréhension, et un dictionnaire unilingue, pour mieux comprendre le mot en contexte.

2 La seconde lecture

- La seconde lecture doit vous mener à établir un résumé de l'action sous forme de fiches qui vous permettront ensuite de vous repérer facilement dans l'œuvre et d'effectuer vos analyses. À la fin de chaque chapitre, répondez à ces questions avec vos propres mots : quels sont les personnages présents dans ce chapitre ? Où sont-ils ? Que leur arrive-t-il ? Qu'ai-je appris de nouveau ? Ajoutez à ce petit résumé une citation qui vous a marqué.
- À partir de votre résumé, dégagez les grands thèmes qui caractérisent l'œuvre : traite-t-elle de l'enfance ? de la guerre ? du voyage ? Ce dernier repérage vous permettra de faire facilement le lien avec les axes du programme.

II Situer l'œuvre dans son contexte

Une œuvre littéraire ne peut être bien comprise et analysée hors de son contexte. Prenez connaissance de la date de publication de l'œuvre, et partez de celle-ci pour mener vos recherches.

1 | Le contexte historique

Commencez par des recherches, par exemple dans une encyclopédie, sur le contexte historique dans lequel l'œuvre s'inscrit. Des **événements historiques marquants** bordent-ils la date de publication de l'ouvrage ? Organisez ces informations sous forme de **frise chronologique**. Prenons l'exemple d'*Alice au pays des merveilles* de Lewis Caroll, publié en 1865.

1817-1901: Reign of **Queen Victoria**. She might have inspired The Queen of Hearts, central character to Alice's adventures.
1859: Darwin's *The Origin of Species*. The pool of tears as well as the dodo that comes out of it might be an allusion to it.
1867: Second Reform Act. *Alice's Adventures in Wonderland* is published at a time of great changes in Britain's political landscape.

2 | Le contexte artistique

Situez l'œuvre dans son contexte artistique. Quels sont les **mouvements littéraires et artistiques marquants** au moment où l'œuvre est publiée ? À quel moment de l'œuvre de l'auteur cet ouvrage paraît-il ?

Didactic nursery rhymes, which were extremely popular during Victoria's reign, are parodied throughout *Alice's Adventures in Wonderland*.
Nonsense literature was on the rise towards the end of the 19th century. Lewis Caroll was one of the authors who popularized it.
Elements of **satire** are present in the novel.

zoOm

Alice's Adventures in Wonderland : Chapter 1

1. **Who are the characters?**
Alice, her sister and the White Rabbit.

2. **Where are they?**
At first, Alice and her sister are sitting on the bank of a river. Then Alice falls into the rabbit-hole, which seems to be a tunnel, but proves to be a strange ditch into which she falls up until she lands in a hall.

3. **What happens to them?**
Alice is with her sister who is reading a book. Then, the White Rabbit catches her attention, and she chases him. The chapter is mostly a description of her eerie fall down the rabbit-hole.

4. **What have I discovered in this chapter?**
It introduces the main character: Alice; and the setting: a strange world where the laws of gravity are challenged.

39 Analyser un roman en lien avec une thématique : *Alice's Adventures in Wonderland*

En bref *Une fois le premier travail d'analyse générale de l'œuvre effectué, vous devrez analyser l'œuvre en fonction des thématiques associées. Ce travail sera amorcé grâce aux extraits étudiés en cours mais vos analyses personnelles seront valorisées lors de la présentation de votre dossier.*

I Associer une œuvre à une thématique

- Ce travail devra être systématique : la référence aux **thématiques** et aux axes d'étude sera essentielle lors de l'épreuve orale pour que votre dossier ne soit pas hors sujet.
- *Alice aux pays des merveilles* peut être associé à **deux thématiques du programme** : « Voyages, territoires, frontières » et « Expression et construction de soi ».

CONSEIL
Lors de l'étude d'une **thématique**, réfléchissez à tous les sens que les termes du sujet peuvent avoir (sens propre, figuré, imagé, etc.).

Voyages, territoires, frontières
- Chute dans le terrier du lapin : voyage spatial
- Arrivée au pays des merveilles : franchissement de la frontière entre le réel et l'imaginaire

Expression et construction de soi
- Âge d'Alice : l'enfance comme moment privilégié pour la construction de soi
- Expression de soi : émancipation d'Alice par la parole, qui lui permet de s'échapper du pays des merveilles
- Péripéties d'Alice : quête de soi qui est le fruit de son inconscient lors de son sommeil

II Choisir un extrait pertinent pour chaque thématique

- L'extrait de votre dossier doit permettre d'exemplifier la thématique présentée. Il faut donc choisir un passage clé de l'œuvre et veiller à sa cohérence : l'importance de l'extrait dans l'œuvre doit être évidente. Il est impératif de montrer que le passage est **emblématique de la thématique**.
- Cela passe par une **explication de texte** dans laquelle il faudra s'appuyer sur tous les éléments de l'extrait : le thème, la tonalité, le style, etc.

zoOm

Alice's Adventures in Wonderland: Expression and construction of the self

This extract from the beginning of Chapter 5 is very important. Alice's 'quest' to find her self begins when she realises that she is changing.

"Who are YOU?" said the Caterpillar.

This was not an encouraging opening for a conversation. Alice replied, rather shyly, "I—I hardly know, sir, just at present—at least I know who I WAS when I got up this morning, but I think I must have been changed several times since then."

"What do you mean by that?" said the Caterpillar sternly. "Explain yourself!"

"I can't explain MYSELF, I'm afraid, sir" said Alice, "because I'm not myself, you see."

"I don't see," said the Caterpillar.

"I'm afraid I can't put it more clearly," Alice replied very politely, "for I can't understand it myself to begin with; and being so many different sizes in a day is very confusing."

"It isn't," said the Caterpillar.

"Well, perhaps you haven't found it so yet," said Alice; "but when you have to turn into a chrysalis—you will some day, you know—and then after that into a butterfly, I should think you'll feel it a little queer, won't you?"

"Not a bit," said the Caterpillar.

"Well, perhaps your feelings may be different," said Alice; "all I know is, it would feel very queer to ME."

Lewis Carroll, *Alice in Wonderland* (1865).

Alice analyses every way in which she has changed. She is a young girl who is growing up- **the passage from childhood to adulthood** is materialised by changes in height.

Instance of **misunderstanding**. As the caterpillar asks Alice to explain herself ("Explain yourself!"), it does not understand the young girl's answer. Alice believes that the caterpillar is asking her to explain who she is, which she proves unable to do since her quest to understand herself has just begun ("I can't explain MYSELF.").

As Alice faces the caterpillar's inability to understand her, she tries to go back to **thinking rationally**, and compares her situation with the caterpillar's. Indeed, the caterpillar itself is about to undergo a similar change and go from childhood to adulthood as it is to become a butterfly.

40 Analyser une œuvre filmique intégrale

En bref *Une analyse filmique ne consiste ni en un résumé, ni en une critique. Il s'agit d'expliquer et justifier les choix du cinéaste. Il faut certes comprendre l'histoire racontée par le film mais aussi analyser les procédés filmiques en s'appuyant sur du vocabulaire technique.*

I Comprendre l'histoire racontée

- Lors du premier visionnement, imprégnez-vous du film, de son atmosphère et des histoires qu'il raconte. Vous pourrez ensuite vous interroger sur votre ressenti. Le film est-il efficace ? difficile ? de quels points de vue ? Quel thème est abordé ? Quels sentiments procure-t-il ?

- Ce qu'il faut observer :

Characters	• appearances and psychological portraits • identities, relationships, goals, quest, competitions, conflicts, trauma, key moments…
Events	• period, dramatic structure and impact, scenes with dialogues, suspense, happy ending or elements of surprise… • key sequences: opening credits, exposition, conclusion, first appearance of a character…
Setting / Dramatisation of space	• place·s, shot on location (*en extérieur*) or on set (*en studio*), open or closed spaces: characters can move freely or they are blocked… • recurring objects, visual symbols connected to a character or not, symbolic or famous places…
Dramatisation of time	• season, weather, daytime or night-time…

II Étudier la narration

1 Analyser les procédés de narration

- Les choix opérés lors du montage déterminent :

• la chronologie des événements : il peut y avoir des analepses (*flashback*) ou des prolepses (*flashforward*) ;

• le rapport entre récit et événements : il peut y avoir des ellipses (*ellipsis*) ou des vitesses différentes (*accelerated motion / slow motion*) ;

• le·s point·s de vue : le narrateur peut être omniscient (*omniscient narrator*) ou faire partie de l'histoire, ce qui a des conséquences sur la nature des informations données.

2 Analyser les procédés de transition

■ Les raccords (transitions entre deux plans contigus) et les différents types de **montage** structurent et ordonnent le récit. Ils créent ainsi un lien dramatique entre deux actions éloignées et simultanées et suscitent des émotions :

- montage court (*fast cutting*) : plans très courts juxtaposés pour créer un effet de rapidité (scènes d'action, de poursuite) ou contracter le temps ;
- montage alterné (*cross-cutting*) : deux actions, à deux endroits différents, montrées en alternance pour souligner leur simultanéité.

VOCABULARY

montage : organisation délibérée des plans d'un film dans certaines conditions d'ordre et de durée. Il révèle les partis-pris du réalisateur.

■ Les plans peuvent être séparés par une coupe franche ou un effet d'optique :

- le fondu (*fade in / out*) est une ponctuation forte entre deux plans, il peut être enchaîné (*dissolve* : passage progressif d'un plan à un autre par la superposition de leurs images) pour créer une transition douce ou au noir (*fade-to-black* : disparition progressive des images jusqu'au noir complet et réapparition de celles-ci) pour faire une courte pause dans le récit ;
- le raccord cut (*cut*) très souvent utilisé, est une coupe brutale entre deux images sans transition. On montre une succession de plans qui s'enchaînent rapidement et plonge brutalement le spectateur dans le plan suivant.

zoom

Parallel editing in *Bloody Sunday*

■ **Parallel editing** (*montage parallèle*) allows two or more related actions occurring at the same time in two separate locations or different points in time to unfold within a single film sequence. It can create tension, show different points of view and it always implies a relationship between the different sets of action.

■ Parallel editing is used at the beginning of the movie *Bloody Sunday*.

Shot 1: Ivan Cooper, leader of the peaceful march, arrives at his Headquarters to hold his press conference.	**Shot 2:** British generals arrive at their Headquarters to hold their press conference.

Effect: right from the beginning we discover two distinct places which are strongly related: discovery of the decision-makers as well as their own stands (*positions*).

41 Analyser un film en lien avec une thématique : *Bloody Sunday*

En bref *L'analyse filmique est intégrée au dossier personnel que vous présenterez à l'oral et doit être rattachée à l'une des thématiques du programme autour de la problématique que vous avez définie.* Bloody Sunday *de Paul Greengrass illustre les thématiques « Arts et débats d'idées » et « Voyages, territoires, frontières ».*

I Illustrating art and debates

- Paul Greengrass has chosen to represent the events and shoot his film like a documentary, often with a handheld camera, so as to produce life-like shaky images, especially in crowd scenes. Besides, some characters even have their backs to the camera and move in and out of frame, as if the cameraman just happened to be there. The soundtrack also has the same true-to-life quality: people can mumble and talk over one another or some noises can supplant voices in conversations. The audience is by those means and effects abruptly confronted to blunt reality.

- The film director adopts the objectivity expected from a journalist: he carefully and faithfully reconstructs the events known as **Bloody Sunday**. Yet, his opting for realism and increasing the impact of images and sounds to arouse strong emotions proves a subtle denunciation of the massacre.

INFO
The film dramatises the peaceful protest march which turned into bloodshed in Derry on January, 30th, 1972 known as **Bloody Sunday**.

- His use of cross-cutting and parallel editing alternately leads the viewer to both camps and thus points at their shared responsibilities in the massacre. The film highlights the necessary conditions to heal past wounds and move on when Bernadette Devlin shouts "We will not rest until justice is done". It definitely supports reconciliation by rejecting partisan attitudes in order to bridge the gap between the two communities as it ends with U2's song.

II Illustrating travels, territories and frontiers

- There are numerous divisions and the use of cross editing points them out; so do the close-ups on the city maps showing the barricades and blocked streets set up by both camps. The yawning chasm is all the more obvious when the marchers sing "We shall overcome" at the end of the press conference while the sound of military drums beats the rhythm of soldiers leaving the room.

- Besides, characters are often isolated in closed spaces like tanks, offices, cars and yards or blocked at the foot of a building as if they were trapped. They can also be unable to react or speak, like Cooper in the hospital scene. This paralysis hints at their inability to change and suggests there is no way out.

The tragic outcome is unavoidable. That's why **fast-cutting** conveys the inevitable and quick chain of events. Confusion and chaos unfold as the shots flow together seamlessly. What's more, the camera follows Cooper and focuses on his back to underline things have come out of hands. The impression is thus given that the march can only lead to rioting and the killing of innocent victims whose names and ages are read at the end of the press conference.

VOCABULARY
fast-cutting: film editing technique which involves several shots of brief duration

zoOm

What is the impact of *Bloody Sunday* by Paul Greengrass?

After the massacre, people's lives changed dramatically in Derry:

- the British Army was totally cleared of any charges and furthermore some soldiers were even decorated;
- the Civil Rights movement was crushed and young Irish men joined the IRA massively.

Thirty years after the tragic events, the film helped raise awareness and trigger changes.

***Bloody Sunday*, 2002**

Art et contestation

In the film Bernadette Devlin says: "We will not rest until justice is done!"

1998-2010. A second inquiry acknowledged the British Army's responsibility in the shooting.

In June 2010, Prime Minister David Cameron addressed apologies on behalf of the British government.

Ancrage et héritage

Paul Greengrass said his film was made "in a spirit of reconciliation to move on."

Non-professional actors were hired, all from Derry and involved in actual events: witnesses, victims' families or descendants and soldiers.

They relived the trauma all together in order to create a sense of unity.

CRÉDITS ICONOGRAPHIQUES

4h © Sherpard Fairey / Obeygiant.com · **4b** ph © Alamy / photo12 · **5** © Stéphane Mattern · **6h** © Stéphane Mattern · **6b** ph © blackred / iStock / Getty-Images Plus · **7** ph © Banksy, photo Auctions / Rex / Shutterstock / Sipa Press · **9** © Sherpard Fairey / Obeygiant.com · **11** ph © Julio Etchart / Alamy / photo12 · **13** ph © B. Christopher / Alamy / photo12 · **15** © Keith Haring Foundation (Collection Noirmont Art Production, Paris) · **17** ph © Estate of Wyndham Lewis / Bridgeman Images, photo Tate, Londres, Dist. RMN-Grand Palais / Tate photography / Bridgeman Images · **19** ph © Elmar Kremser/Sven Simon/Picture-Alliance /AFP · **21** ph © Working Title / The Kobal Collection / Aurimages · **22** ph © tomeng / iStockphoto · **23** ph © Olga Popova / Shutterstock · **25** ph © Estate of Wyndham Lewis / Imperial War Museum / Bridgeman Images · **37** © Sheila Rock · **39** ph © Art Collection 2 / Alamy / photo12 · **41** ph © Banksy, photo Auctions / Rex / Shutterstock / Sipa Press · **43** ph © Apatow Productions / HBO / BBQ_DFY / Aurimages · **45** ph © Heritage Images / Fine Art Images / photo12 · **47** ph © Imperial War Museum, © IWM / Aurimages · **49** ph © Ifc Productions / Detour Filmproduction / The Kobal Collection / Aurimage · **50** © Asher Brown Durand, The Beeches, 1845, MET · **51** © Vincent van Gogh Self-Portrait with a Straw Hat (The Potato Peeler), 1887, MET · **55** © Sheila Rock · **63** © Isabelle Kherbouche · **65** ph © Bonhams, London, UK / Bridgeman Images · **67** © Max Standley Trail of Tears courtesy R. Michelson Galleries · **69** ph © Reporters Associés / Gamma – Rapho · **71** ph © Alamy / photo12 · **73** © Image courtesy of the National Archives of Australia. · **75** © Kimathi Donkor · **76** © MET · **77** ph © Moussa81 / Getty-Images / iStock Editorial LD · **79** © Gene Luen Yang © Macmillan Publishers · **91** ph © Christophe Morin / Pix Palace · **93** © Stéphane Mattern · **103** ph © Tierney – stock.adobe.com · **109** ph © The Granger Coll NY / Aurimages · **121** © Stéphane Mattern · **139** © Stéphane Mattern · **155** © Stéphane Mattern · **167** © 2002 Bórd Scannán na hÉireann / Granada Television / Hell's Kitchen Films / Portman Entertainment Group / Screen Ireland · **170h** ph © George Sweeney / Alamy / photo12 · **170b** ph © Paul Faith / AFP photo · **183** ph © blackred / iStock / Getty-Images Plus · **189** © 2002 Bórd Scannán na hÉireann / Granada Television / Hell's Kitchen Films / Portman Entertainment Group / Screen Ireland

PAPIER À BASE DE FIBRES CERTIFIÉES

Hatier s'engage pour l'environnement en réduisant l'empreinte carbone de ses livres. Celle de cet exemplaire est de :
700 g éq. CO_2
Rendez-vous sur www.hatier-durable.fr

Achevé d'imprimer en Italie par L.E.G.O. S.p.A.
Dépôt legal n° 06459-1/01 – Août 2020